THE
LEADERSHIP
ADVANTAGE

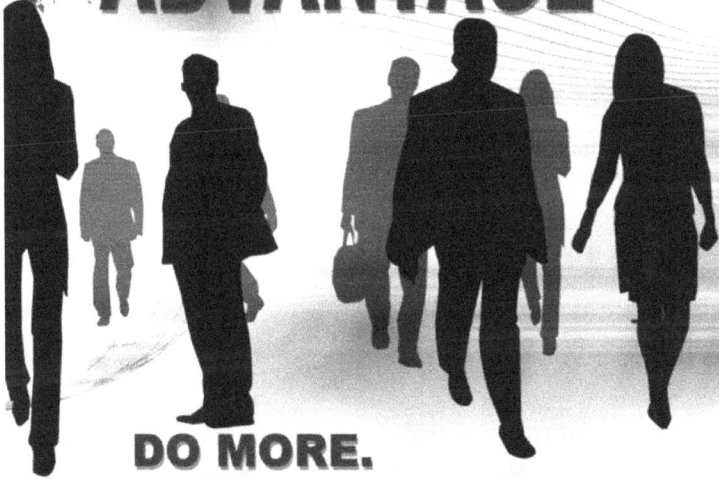

DO MORE.
LEAD MORE.
EARN MORE.

Ervin (Earl) Cobb

Acclaim for Earl Cobb and *The Leadership Advantage*

"The *Leadership Advantage* serves as an evaluative guidepost for aspiring and seasoned professionals seeking to increase their engagement and effectiveness as leaders."

- Dr. Rufus Glasper, Chancellor, Maricopa Community Colleges

"I personally had the opportunity to see Earl Cobb grow over the years to become a Vice President of the company. To do this, he had to have all of the attributes to be a great leader. So he writes from experience."

- Napoleon Hornbuckle, Corporate Vice President (Retired), Motorola

"Mr. Cobb has captured the pure essence of Leadership in this work. His broad based experience guides his insight in every topical area."

- Albert L. McHenry, Ph.D. Vice President and Executive Vice Provost, Arizona State University

"Earl Cobb has done it again with his new book, *The Leadership Advantage*. Earl is that rarest of authors. He writes with the power of someone who has been there."

- Doug Russell, Vice President of Operations, Lean Leadership Institute

"This is a great publication on leadership. The 10 attributes of should resonate with anyone who has a desire to leave a valued legacy of being an influence in business & society. I fully endorse this publication and believe it can change your life."

- Morris Daniely, Director Quality Engineering, Honeywell Process Solutions, Global Technology Quality Assurance

"Mr. Cobb is the walking definition of Leadership. Strong, Wise, and Dedicated are only a few words to describe his leadership abilities. I am a big fan of his work."

- Cory Simpson, Financial Advisor, Merrill Lynch

"Earl Cobb has written a practical and insightful guide to mastering the leadership mindset. *The Leadership Advantage* transcends the business world and is useful in gaining a greater understanding and development of one's own personal potential."

- Michael Searles, Ph.D., Emeritus Professor, Georgia Regents University, Co-Editor of *Buffalo Soldiers in the West*

"*The Leadership Advantage* takes the reader "step by step" through the 10 most important goals for anyone striving to become better."

- Sally Wurr, President, SW Insurance Corp and SW Ventures Group

"Earl Cobb's Absolute Attributes belong on every leader's desk. Read this book, embrace the message and become the leader you can be."

- Jim Grigsby, President/CEO, Jim Grigsby Consulting, Author of *Don't Tick Off the Gators*

"*The Leadership Advantage: Do More, Lead More, Earn More*, is a great book. A must read book for both men and women alike who are looking to be better than they are, greater than they are and accomplish more than they ever thought possible. Read this book and the world will open up for you."

- Tony Rose, Publisher, Amber Books, Author of *America: The Black Point of View*

"Interesting and helpful. I would like all of my brokers to read it."

Ann Anovitz, Chairman, Ann Anovitz Associates, Commercial Real Estate

"Entrepreneurs, who want to start, sustain and scale their businesses, should read Earl Cobb's book."

Franne McNeal, President, Significant Business Results, LLC, Author of *Significant! From Frustrated to FranneTastic*

"Earl Cobb provides an excellent overview of the key attributes of personal and professional leadership. From presence to focus to clarity, he outlines in a practical manner what leaders and those aspiring to become leaders can do to lead more and earn more by maximizing their *Leadership Advantage*."

- Dr. Fay Cobb Payton, Associate Professor, Information Systems & Technology, NC State University and Author of *Leveraging Intersectionality: Seeing and Not Seeing.*

"This book is written with such clarity and detail that anyone reading it and following Mr. Cobb's advice is sure to make a success of them self in whatever venture they undertake. His wisdom, common sense and sincerity are projected all through the book."

- Dr. Marilou McIntyre, Author/Publisher, Author of *The Forever Principles: Listening to an Angel Voice in my Head*

"Earl Cobb nailed it on the head when he wrote: "presence is the radiance of authenticity". From my very first contact with Mr. Cobb, I felt his strong presence, his earnestness and his strength as a leader. In his new book, *The Leadership Advantage*, Mr. Cobb does a remarkable job identifying and offering the reader the ten absolute attributes required for leadership and how to master them for oneself. His new book is not only authentic, it also radiates brilliance. A must read for anyone desiring to master leadership."

- Dr. Susan R. Cushing, DMD and Author of *Fat No More! The Book of Hope for Losing Weight*

"Written from practical experience and success. An inspiration!"

Robert Bunnett, Senior Vice President of Innovation, SM&A

"Mr. Cobb will take you on an amazing journey through leadership tenets. His work should be read by anyone aspiring to lead. Enhance your leadership quotient...enhance your life!"

- Kenneth Morton, Management Associate, Information Technology Senior Management Forum

Also By Ervin (Earl) Cobb

Focused Leadership
What You Can Do Today To Become a More Effective Leader

God's Goodness and Our Mindfulness
Responding Versus Reacting to Life Changing Circumstances

Pillow Talk Consciousness
Intimate Reflections on America's 100
Most Interesting Thoughts and Suspicions

Living a Richer Life
Getting the Most out of Life's Gifts and Circumstances

Navigating the Life Enrichment Model™

Published and Distributed by ⊭RICHER Press
An Imprint of Richer Life, LLC

The Leadership Advantage: Do More. Lead More. Earn More.

First Edition, April 2015

Cover Design: Richer Media USA
Photographs: Richer Media USA and Big Stock Photo

Library of Congress Cataloging-in-Publications Data
2015938110
Cobb, Ervin (Earl)
The Leadership Advantage: Do More. Lead More. Earn More
1. Management 2. Leadership 3. Reference

ISBN 13: 978-0-9863544-6-5
ISBN 10: 0986354465

CONTENTS

CONTENTS

PREFACE

Understanding the
Leadership Advantage

What do all of the following descriptors have in common?

Charismatic	Pace Setter
Innovative	Servant
Command and Control	Situational
Laissez-Faire	Transformational

Well, they are all terms commonly used today to describe leadership and/or leadership styles. You will also see leadership defined as an ability, a collective action, an act, a skill, a capacity, a process and even the office or position of a leader. We currently perceive our leaders as being autocratic, participative, democratic, task oriented, transitional or even true. Cross-culturally, it has been determined that there are perhaps several hundred leadership theories, including the Great Man theories, Behavioral theories and Trait-based theories.

Without question, leadership is one of the most studied, documented, discussed, celebrated and sometimes mystifying subjects that mankind has encountered. This apparent confusion and/or transformation of leadership theories has been going on for centuries, as revealed in the philosophical writings from Plato's Republic. Yet still, none of us can escape the fact that we spend most of our lives either leading or being led.

As professionals, we all, to some degree, can reflect back over the years and list numerous leadership roles that we either accepted or were given as we progressed in our careers. Like many of you, over my professional and management career, I have had the privilege to serve in many somewhat diverse leadership roles. My list includes: leading technology development as a young computer engineer in the 70s; leading major equipment manufacturing projects as a manager in the 80s; leading large business teams within Fortune 100 companies as an executive in the 90s; and leading a venture capital backed internet start-up as well as family-financed entrepreneurial business franchises in the early 2000s.

And to think, we could include in such lists the demanding civic, community and charitable board positions which challenged every ounce of leadership experience gained from our professional endeavors. Other than just reminding me that Father Time is quickly passing me by, this *broader view of leadership* was the catalyst that ignited my long-time interest in writing *"The Leadership Advantage: Do More. Lead More. Earn More."*

I am well aware that my list of *reflections* on the types of experiences I have had is very similar to millions of other professionals who have had long, diverse careers in all kinds of industries. However, as an author who writes about leadership, I have a tendency to *scratch anything that itches*. Within the apparent confusion and/or transformation of leadership at this early point of the 21st century and with some new insights recently gained from my role as an adjunct professor of leadership at the post-graduate level, I have been moved to ask the question, *"Was my success and my rewards based primarily on me leading others or on me, first, becoming a good leader of myself?"*

I recall once hearing that when you learn to be a *good leader of yourself,* you also learn how to be a good person, a good husband or wife, a good father or mother, a good student, a good teacher and a good communicator. In the normal progression of one's career where *opportunity* and *experience* are the enablers of more *opportunity* and more *experience*, maybe a good *leader of self* also evolves into a good conflict manager, a good goal setter, a good planner, a good coach and *eventually* a good leader of others.

As research for the book, I spent about a year simply asking people the question, "What comes first to your mind when you hear the word leadership?" I was not surprised to learn that most of us think of leadership in terms of *people* or *groups of people* [our leadership] or those applying leadership knowledge and skills within governments, companies, organizations, groups, teams, etc. *as a process* [our leaders]. The other thing that rang consistently true was that almost everyone I asked stressed the need for a good leader to have faithful followers, to be able to articulate a purpose or mission and to know what is to be achieved or earned when victory is won. However, no one mentioned the need for a good leader to *first* be a good leader of his or her self.

In *The Leadership Advantage: Do More. Lead More. Earn More.* I explore the concept that leadership is indeed a "verb" and a powerful professional competency that is anchored by what I call *Absolute Attributes.* I also describe how these attributes innately touch every aspect of our lives, our relationships and our professions.

The book's concise discussions and explorations build the premise that by strengthening the *primary set* of attributes which comprise your unique inner-being, you will gain an advantage over

The Leadership Advantage

those who think of leadership as something that others do or merely as a process. This perspective and the strategic use of your *primary attributes* will become your *Leadership Advantage*. Simply stated --- you will come to appreciate that the more you do to lead yourself, *[through your ideas, thoughts, opinions and points of view]* the more *[recognition, acknowledgment, respect and rewards]* you will earn.

In the book, I discuss in detail each of the *Ten Absolute Attributes of Leadership* which create the framework for gaining the *Leadership Advantage*. In addition, I articulate specific goals you should pursue to ensure that your *primary set* of attributes maximizes your Leadership Advantage.

The "*Leader-In-You*" and "*Selfish-Food-For-Thought*" exercises presented at the end of book have been proven to be valuable in identifying a leader's primary attributes. The goal is to assist you achieve your highest level of career, business and personal successes by helping you maximize your *Leadership Advantage*.

"We shall not cease from exploration, and the end of all our exploring will be to arrive where we started and know the place for the first time."

— T. S. Eliot, *American essayist, publisher, playwright, literary and social critic*

Exploring the Leadership Advantage

In the following ten chapters, we will explore a distinctive perspective on leadership. This more expansive way of viewing leadership and situationally adapting a core set of inherent leadership attributes can help all of us improve our professional performance and success in many aspects of our lives.

From this perspective, you will quickly begin to view leadership as a *verb* and appreciate its power as a strategic professional competency. Exploring this concept will expand your understanding and your ability to consciously employ the inherent human traits which embody "leadership" in its most complete form, called the *Ten Absolute Attributes of Leadership*.

Just as a verb is the most important part of a sentence, leadership can become the most important part of influencing the activities required to accomplish important goals in both your personal and professional life. Leading is not something you observe. Leading is something you do.

As mentioned in the Preface, this broader perspective of leadership and the strategic use of your *primary leadership attributes* will become your *Leadership Advantage*. As you gain this prospective, I contend that you will come to appreciate what millions of very successful leaders have learned...that is, the more you do to lead yourself, *[through your ideas, thoughts, opinions and points of view]* the more *[recognition, acknowledgment, respect and rewards]* you will earn.

Each of the following chapters will give you the opportunity to closely explore one of the *Ten Absolute Attributes of Leadership* and how they can influence and shape the most desired and most successful outcomes. The *"Leader-In-You"* and *"Selfish-Food-For-Thought" exercises* presented at the end of the book can help identify your primary attributes and maximize your Leadership Advantage.

Before we began our exploration, let's first briefly examine the centuries old concept of leader traits and attributes and overview the practical method by which *The Ten Absolute Attributes* were selected from among dozens of documented leadership traits.

Leader Traits and Attributes

A trait, of course, is what we call a characteristic way in which an individual perceives, feels, believes and acts. An attribute is an inherent characteristic or quality.

For centuries, pioneers of the field of human psychology and personality assessment have documented the most important leadership traits of their times based on theories, studies and observations. During your academic studies you most likely have come across many such lists of leadership attributes. Perhaps you have also studied the works of Erik Erikson, Abraham Maslow, Hans Eysenck, Robert White, Sigmond Freud, Albert Bandura and Carl Rogers. From Erikson's stages of psychosocial development to Maslow's famous theories of motivation to Rogers humanistic approach to personality they all put forward their contemporary explanation of observations and behaviors. The question of how leaders differ from non-leaders is one of the oldest in psychology, yet it remains a source of disagreement and controversy among leadership scholars today.

In academia and contemporary literature, there are those who believe that leaders are born. This group is convinced that there are certain leadership attributes that are natural qualities possessed by only a very few people. While others believe that most people who do not naturally possess these leadership qualities can acquire them through diligent training and self-control.

In my studies of leaders and leadership traits over the past 30 years, as a student, a corporate executive and a teacher, it appears that with the exception of a few mega personalities who stand out above the rest, most leaders cling to a somewhat traditional set of widely-touted leadership attributes or qualities.

Whether inherent or acquired, they tend to employ a specific set of attributes in a fashion similar to someone they have known, read about or admire. I am sure you can easily recognize the most common of these leadership attributes. Depending on a particular type of organization, environment or circumstance, a typical set of attributes would most likely include:

- Honesty
- Responsibility
- Confidence
- Enthusiasm
- Motivation
- Reliability
- Decisiveness
- Determination
- Loyalty and
- Courage.

The Leadership Advantage

All of which are admirable and sound human traits.

Although research shows that the possession of certain attributes alone does not guarantee leadership success, there is evidence that the most effective and enduring leaders do differ from other leaders in at least one obvious way. It appears that the most effective leaders have a distinct advantage in the ease in which they deploy their strongest leadership attributes. They also seem to consistently achieve both personal and professional success. They tend to get more leadership opportunities, win more of the battles in the trenches and earn more recognition, acknowledgment, respect and rewards.

How do they do this? What comprises their primary set of leadership attributes? Why does there appear to be a strong relationship between their personal achievements and their professional achievements? What anchors the apparent trust, confidence and absoluteness when it comes to selecting, adapting and deploying certain leadership attributes?

These and other pertinent questions will be addressed in the following chapters as we continue our exploration of the Leadership Advantage.

The Ten Absolute Attributes of Leadership

While pondering many of the questions presented in the previous section and reviewing dozens of studies, articles and research reports, I finally was able to generate a list of thirty-seven leadership attributes which appeared most often in published literature. I closely examined and ranked each attribute based on what my research and my real-world experience supported as the human traits most fundamental and absolute when it comes to effective 21st century leadership. At that point, I reduced the list down to the top ten attributes.

Although many other traits have been associated with successful and effective leaders, those selected as the *Ten Absolute Attributes of Leadership* are as follows:

- ¤ Presence
- ¤ Vision
- ¤ Clarity
- ¤ Persistence
- ¤ Motivation
- ¤ Unselfishness
- ¤ Deliberation
- ¤ Courage
- ¤ Respect; and
- ¤ Focus.

The Leadership Advantage

While all of the of the attributes studied could be described as worthy leadership traits, it was found that there were a couple of very distinctive and significant facets regarding this particular set of attributes as compared to most of the others.

First, each of the *Ten Absolute Attributes of Leadership* seems to encompass an inherent human characteristic that most people possess to some extent. Each of the attributes seems to find its way, at some point, into every professional's "successful leader" toolkit. Each attribute represents a distinct personal trait. Each trait is capable of being strengthened, lessened and even discounted based on the value an individual places on its innate existence and the numerous situations, environments and circumstances encountered through his or her life.

As professionals...

- ¤ We all have some level of presence. When we walk into a room, we will be noticed.
  However, do we always know by whom and to what degree?

- ¤ We all depend on a plan, a road map or a vision to know what to do next or what to expect at the end of a journey.

  But, how broad and how deep is our visioning and can it be effectively communicated to others?

¤ We all have learned that a significant part of being viewed as a professional depends on our ability to clearly express ourselves verbally and in writing.

But, then again, does our clarity present itself as sufficiently lucent and transparent when the situation demands it?

¤ We all have exhibited a level of persistence in order to have achieved our current position in life.

But, how closely is our "dogged persistence" tied to long-term and trusted endurance?

¤ We all have been motivated by something or someone at multiple-points in our lives and our careers.

However, does the impetus of our motivation come with a lot of overhead and can it be easily translated into a source for stimulating others?

¤ We all have learned that being an effective team member requires a degree of compromise and unselfishness.

But, can we always balance what may be perceived as unselfishness or bigheartedness with what can also be interpreted as a weakness?

¤ We all have some ability to be thoughtful and deliberate.

But, how can we prevent "too much deliberation" or the lack of deliberation from negatively impacting our ability to reach our goals.

¤ We all have some mental or moral strength to persevere and withstand danger, fear, or difficulty.

However, because courage is required in almost every basic human activity or endeavor, how do we ration our courageousness consistent with the results that can be expected?

¤ We all desire to be respected and we understand its value in getting things done through others.

But, are we capable of consistently giving the proper level of respect to situations and circumstances as well as to individuals?

¤ We all have some ability to direct our attention to events and activities when it is apparent that there is a need or a problem.

However, do we have the natural instinct or sufficient skill to proactively plant strategic and tactical markers to ensure that the proper focus is always where it needs to be?

The second distinctive and significant facet regarding this particular set of attributes is the realization that collectively, they embody what many people in today's business world are seeking in a leader --- both as a superior and as a person.

Most of today's contemporary literature describes an effective leader as someone who is not only capable of inspiring others but also has the attributes required to cultivate a broad and deep level of trust throughout an organization. He or she must also be competent at coordinating and collaborating among the many different and diverse resources which reside throughout the organization. When a leader possesses a strong combination and a high degree of personal attributes such as presence, clarity, unselfishness and respectfulness, he or she will find it significantly easier to cultivate trust and rely on others.

The understanding of the *collective significance* of these ten attributes combined with the recognition that most of us possess all these inherent human characteristics, to some extent, makes the opportunity of gaining a Leadership Advantage available to all of us.

I would suggest that the probability of any one being born with what might be considered a *maximum level* of all ten attributes is fairly small. However, most professionals who have achieved a leadership position most likely possess at least an *average level* of all ten of these attributes. As illustrated in the diagram on the next page, by increasing your innate levels of each attribute, you can elevate yourself to a higher position on the opportunity scale. This increase in position should also equate to an increase in *Leadership Advantage.*

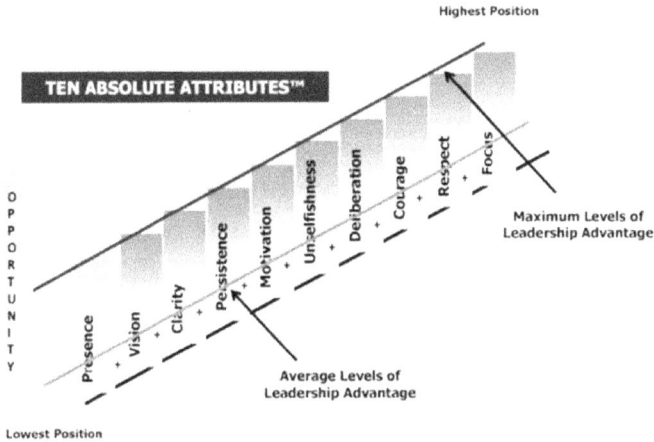

In the following chapters we explore opportunities for increasing innate levels of each *Absolute Attribute* and provide specific insight into the personal and professional goals you should pursue to allow each of the *Ten Absolute Attributes* to play its role in helping you maximize your Leadership Advantage.

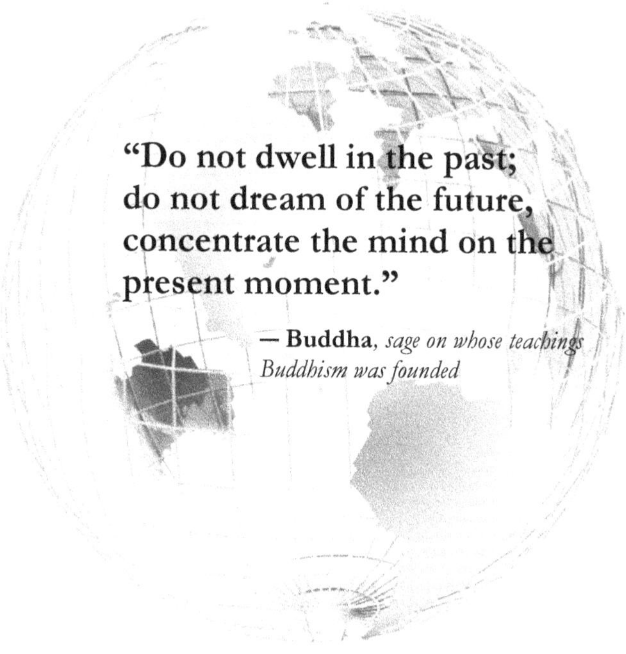

"Do not dwell in the past;
do not dream of the future,
concentrate the mind on the
present moment."

— **Buddha**, *sage on whose teachings
Buddhism was founded*

CHAPTER ONE
LEADERSHIP AND
PRESENCE

"If your mind carries a heavy burden of past, you will experience more of the same. The past perpetuates itself through lack of presence. The quality of your consciousness at this moment is what shapes the future."

— Eckhart Tolle, *German-born writer and speaker*

The Leadership Advantage

As professionals, we all have some level of *presence*. When we walk into a room, we will be noticed. However, do we always know by whom and to what degree?

In order to gain a better understanding of how the traits associated with your *presence,* as an individual and a leader, influences outcomes and what you can do to enhance your innate presence, we will explore the following:

¤ What is *presence* and why it is a major factor when it comes to successfully *leading yourself* and leading others?

¤ How can you develop or enhance your command of *presence?* and

¤ What is the primary role of *presence* in establishing and maintaining a leadership advantage?

The Power of Presence

Personal presence is not easy to define, but we all know it when we see it. Every one notices it when you walk into a room. Almost on cue, heads turn and people step aside. Regardless of the subject being discussed, the conversation opens up to include you. When you speak everyone listens. When you ask a question, someone is always there with an answer.

The same is true with what can be called *leadership presence*. Leadership presence can be thought of as the ability to do at least a couple of things very well. The first is to demonstrate your worth, whether to one person or to hundreds of thousands of people, in an authentic way. The second is to connect well with your stakeholders. This requires being authentic, comfortable in your own skin and being able to get your message across to everyone who should find it important.

Similar to the adage, "charity starts at home", developing a strong command of our leadership presence also starts at home. Because presence is the radiance of authenticity, it is a major factor when it comes to leading yourself and leading others.

Home is the place where we radiate the most sincerity and learn what it takes to make good things happen on a consistent basis. Leading ourselves to recognize and appreciate presence, starts with recognizing and appreciating who we are as an individual and as a leader.

As a business leader in today's environment of global commerce and social media, you have literally hundreds of interpersonal interactions each and every day. If at any time you fail to instill confidence among subordinates and peers, you may lose their loyalty, harm their morale and hinder their ability to execute.

The impact, reach and power of presence is not only limited to your co-workers, but to everyone with whom you come in contact with throughout the day and every day. Your presence or lack thereof, as an individual and a leader, can be a major factor in your relationships at work and at home.

You should remember that your *presence* is an *Absolute Attribute*. That is, presence is vital to what completes you as an individual. Your personal presence feeds your professional presence and they both come from within and are under your control. By strategically elevating your leadership presence and using it in concert with your other *Absolute Attributes*, you can take your influence as a leader to a whole, new level.

Enhancing Command of Presence

Some leaders happen upon the skill of commanding their presence naturally, while others have to work very hard to develop it. While there are many things that lead to developing a strong "command presence", a focus on developing the following three areas will have an immediate impact on enhancing your command presence.

1. Be Trustworthy and Show People You Care

When you closely examine the characteristics of what really constitutes effective leadership and distinguishes truly effective leaders from all others, you will find that it is not power, not a title, not authority or not even technical competency.

Instead, what sets you apart is your ability to earn and keep both the loyalty and trust of those whom you lead. Strong leadership presence will allow you to easily project your trust worthiness, your humility and your concern for the welfare of others.

When you take the time to build strong relationships with those you lead, you can more easily earn their trust and loyalty. This sort of human and business connection will allow you to span positional and philosophical gaps, survive mistakes, challenges, downturns and other obstacles that will inevitably occur.

2. Develop Great Verbal Skills

As you are most likely aware, you began developing great verbal skills with developing great listening skills. You must try to understand before you will be understood. When it is time to speak, you should say what you mean and mean what you say. What you say, when you say it and how you say it will either spawn confidence as well as serve to motivate and inspire, or it will take the wind right out of your sails. It is not necessary to be long-winded. You should just be measured and articulate. Remember, that as the leader, a "whisper" may be perceived by some subordinates as a "roar". It is very difficult to lead if you cannot communicate with clarity and with ease.

3. Make Good Decisions

Nothing is more detrimental for you as a leader than a poor track record. Your ability to layer solid decision upon solid decision is crucial to creating loyalty. Making good decisions not only instills confidence. It is also the best way to lead. Your track record of good decisions is an example for those you lead. A track record of making good decisions does not take long to become part of your reputation, which provides you with a heightened level of trust, respect and leadership presence even prior to entering a room.

The bottom line is that if you develop a strong command presence, becoming a more effective and admired leader becomes easier.

Presence and the Leadership Advantage

Presence is a unique competence and fundamental to the concept of *Leadership Advantage*. As we all know, competence is best defined as possessing the skill and knowledge required to *take the action* necessary to ensure successful outcomes. Competence also describes our ability to apply prior experience to new situations with good result. The competency associated with your presence usually increases over time as you acquire more life experience.

Presence is the leadership attribute which creates the groundwork necessary to maximize the influence of all the other *Absolute Attributes*. A strong case can be made that once you are viewed as having strong professional presence --- i.e. being in the moment, possessing a cadre of positive relationships throughout your organization, perceived as being a passionate communicator and a truly authentic individual --- maximizing the influence of the other nine *Absolute Attributes* becomes a much easier task.

With a strong command of your presence, your *vision* is better understood. Your written and verbal communications take on a special level of

The Leadership Advantage

clarity. Your *persistence* becomes contagious. Your ability to *motivate* others becomes effortless.

The following diagram summarizes the personal goals you should pursue to enable *presence* to play a role in helping you maximize your Leadership Advantage.

Average Level of Presence	Maximum Level of Presence
You respond to most situations in a consistent and familiar manner.	You act in the moment and you are flexible enough to handle the unexpected.
You allow your relationships to develop based on the individual and perceived value to you.	You build relationships through empathy, listening and authentic connections.
You convey most of your messages with clarity and clear authority.	You express feelings and emotions while delivering one congruent message.
You adjust your responses and actions based on who you are around.	You accept yourself, you are authentic and you reflect your values in your actions.
	The Leadership Advantage

"Real generosity towards the
future lies in giving all to the
present."

—**Albert Camus,** *French
Nobel Prize winning author,
journalist, and philosopher*

CHAPTER TWO

LEADERSHIP AND
VISION

"A leader's role is to raise people's aspirations for what they can become and to release their energies so they will try to get there."

— David Gergen, *American political commentator and former presidential advisor*

We all depend on a plan, a road map or a vision to know what to do next or what to expect at the end of a journey. But, how broad and how deep is our visioning and can it be effectively communicated to others?

In order to explore the relationship between "leadership" and "vision" and reveal possible opportunities for a *leadership advantage*, we must remove ourselves from the idea that all leaders have vision and that the very essence of leadership is to have the ability to articulate a vision. By removing ourselves from this fundamentally sound but practically suspect premise, we are left with the need to start our exploration by taking a closer look at the art of visioning and then gaining a broader view of how this powerful attribute can be practically deployed beyond simply sharing a dream or painting a picture for others.

So, let's briefly explore:

¤ What is the art of visioning and why do some do it better than others?

- ¤ How you can leverage this attribute beyond telling a passionate story?

- ¤ What advantage you will gain by becoming a more skilled "visioneer" in all aspects of your life?

The Art of Visioning

During his 1992 presidential re-election campaign, President George H. W. Bush alluded to how he did not know what "the vision-thing" was all about. He lost. In contrast, his opponent said that he had a clear vision of a revitalized America. He won.

While it is certain that vision is not the whole story, the outcome re-affirmed the wisdom of Proverbs 29:18: "Where there is no vision, the people perish." I believe that this is true of any undertaking where the hearts and minds of others, as well as yourself, are the most important ingredients of success. But, as we shall see in this chapter, a vision is more than the inspiration of a visionary leader. Your vision must also include the details of execution that create clear direction and understanding. This is why I also believe that visioning is an art.

Most dictionaries define vision as the "power of discerning future conditions; shrewdness in planning and foresight." To some extent, we all have such power. Some of us are more inherently capable than others to look into the future, whether it is next year or next week and plan for certain outcomes. However, the main challenge associated with successfully achieving your "visions" is not the lack of inherent visionary capability. Rather, it is about understanding and acquiring the skills of articulating and leveraging this important leadership attribute to your advantage.

The art of visioning enables us to move forward with clarity. It links the specific business or personal objectives and targets with our core values. The process also helps us to define a plan that we can use to guide us to successfully achieving our goals. It is a process that speaks directly to the need for an inspiring yet detailed vision for both professional and personal success.

The following six steps provide a framework for touching most of the bases associated with crafting a vision to help guide you through a current business or personal situation.

1. Capture the Current Situation

Where are you today and where do you need to be in the future? In this step you should not ignore what is happening around you today nor should you work in isolation. Utilize friends, acquaintances and family members to help you honestly gain an awareness of your present state.

Your appraisal should include all of the advantages and disadvantages.

2. Define the Best Outcome

What can you expect to achieve? In this step, it is important to evaluate all of your options based on a "realistic" assessment. Then, select the best outcome that can be realized with the level of risk you are willing to accept. This selection will translate into your goal and where you expect to land when all is said and done. It is, in effect, your vision.

3. Embrace the Importance of the Outcome

Why is this important to you? At times, we may create a vision for ourselves or our organization which is more of a fad or something you must do because everyone else is doing it. Defining a vision or goal without understanding and truly embracing why it is important to you or your organization is meaningless.

4. Determine the Obstacles to Achieving Success

Who or what is in your way? Determining what you need or where you want to be, can be a success in its own right. However, knowing how to get there and doing it is the ultimate challenge. It is useful to identify in a proactive manner the possible obstacles that you foresee in the way to achieving your vision. These obstacles may be geographic, may be related to people or to financial resources or even environmental factors that could adversely impact your actions.

5. **Determine the Actions to Overcome all Obstacles**

What will you do and when? This is a crucial step. Identifying the appropriate and available actions required to reach your vision is paramount to your success. Determining the changes that are clearly within your control and can be initiated early is very important. Selecting a set of actions that are "appropriate" and "available" is the most important part of the execution. Otherwise, without them the vision remains a dream.

6. **Set Priorities and Monitor Result**

Have you properly laid the groundwork for the next set of actions? Are you on track to achieve your ultimate goal? It is tempting to try to change everything at once. Prudence dictates that you work on the basis of defined priorities. Without priorities, you could squander valuable resources, time and effort in working on relatively less important actions. You should monitor your results against stated actions and track your progress towards achieving your vision.

Leverage Visioning Beyond Passionate Storytelling

Over the years, I have discovered that there are two elements common to all effective visions: 1) they are all implemented and 2) they all yield the planned results. This is true regardless of whether the vision targets professional or personal goals.

As I mentioned earlier, leadership has many definitions and many valuable components or attributes. "Vision" has been selected as one the *Absolute Attributes* in the context of the Leadership Advantage for four primary reasons. When we subject ourselves to the art of the visioning process, we go beyond enhancing our professional ability to tell a good story. We also ignite our personal and natural tendencies for *reflection*, *socialization*, *experimentation* and *observation*.

Here are some thoughts to keep in mind around the power of visioning in connection with your Leadership Advantage.

- ¤ **Reflection** - A vision of any type can only be developed when you take time away to reflect and slow down.

- ¤ **Socialization** - The planning and execution of a vision must involve others for two reasons. First, none of us are fully self-sufficient. We are, as humans, built to be interdependent on one another. Second, we have a hard time seeing what is exceptional within us and we need others to point that out.

¤ **Experimentation** - Visions that have tangible, positive and lasting results are cultivated when we experiment within our areas of interests and gifting. We learn more about ourselves by doing.

¤ **Observation** - Honing a professional or personal vision requires good self-awareness and tracking our responses to the various experiments we conduct.

The Advantages of Becoming a Skilled "Visioneer"

There are advantages you can gain by becoming a more skilled visioneer in all aspects of your life. Here are just a few:

¤ Visioning is the first step in crafting strategic and achievable plans for your career, family and your life.

¤ A well-crafted vision that is shared by all the members of your family and/or your business or company can help everyone involved to assist in the advancement and achievement of your goals.

⌐ A vision brings meaning to what you do every day. It can mobilize others to support you with action and not just words.

⌐ A vision can grab people and then bring them into the fold.

As a skilled visioneer, you are able to craft effective visions. An effective vision strikes a chord in people. It motivates them by tapping their competitive drive. It arouses desire for greatness or interest in doing the right thing. It tantalizes them with personal gain. It appeals to their need to make a difference in the world. When your vision is effective and strong, all of your stakeholders get caught up in what you are doing. They absorb the vision, and commit themselves to your goals and your values.

The following diagram summarizes the personal goals you should pursue to enable *vision* to play a role in helping you maximize your Leadership Advantage.

The Leadership Advantage

Average Level of Vision	Maximum Level of Vision
You quickly sense your situation without a thorough review.	You take the time to capture all aspects of the situation.
You assume that the outcome is the best available to you.	You define the best outcome and know why it is important to you and your goals.
You do what you feel is necessary and hope everything works out.	You identify the appropriate and available actions required to reach your vision.
You take advantage of the opportunities that surface to move you toward your goals.	You set priorities, monitor results closely and lay the groundwork for the next set of actions.
	The Leadership Advantage

"For those who confuse
you, recognize that their
confusion is theirs and your
clarity is yours."

— Barbara Marciniak,
*inspirational speaker and best-selling
author*

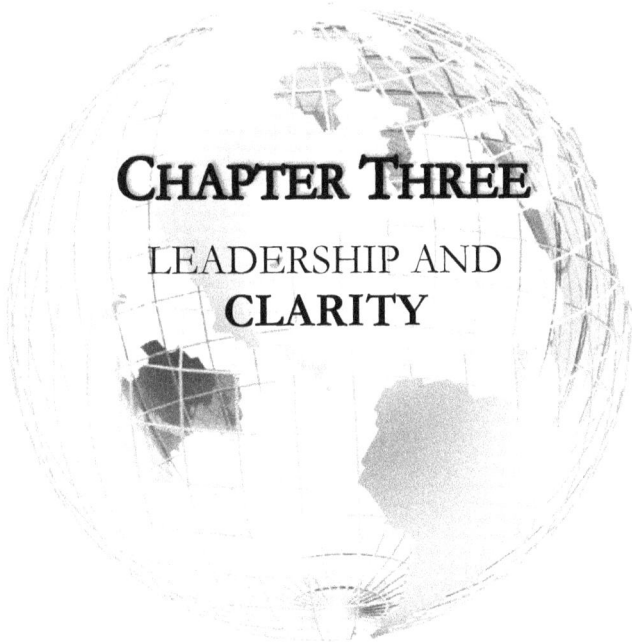

CHAPTER THREE

LEADERSHIP AND
CLARITY

"For me the greatest beauty always lies in the greatest clarity."

— Gotthold Ephraim Lessing,
*German writer, philosopher,
dramatist, publicist and art critic*

We all have learned that a significant part of being viewed as a professional depends on our ability to clearly express ourselves verbally and in writing. Both verbal and written communications are essential for effective business and personal expression. Clarity leads to effective communication.

While there are many subtleties to the verbal communication between people, some basic skills can help you leverage this key attribute to become a more effective communicator. In order to have reached the success you have reached in both your personal and professional life, you are most likely already a good communicator. I have found that we all can improve the *clarity* of our communications in any situation by becoming more cognizant of some natural communications barriers.

These barriers fall into the following camps:

- ¤   Barriers to Listening;
- ¤   Barriers to Accurate Perception; and

¤　Barriers to Effective Verbal Communication

In this chapter we will explore these three barriers as well as some suggested strategies for effectively addressing them.

Barriers to Listening

The following are examples of some barriers to listening which have a tendency to interfere with the clarity of our communications. They are actions or situations that you should be keenly aware of and development methods to eliminate and/or control. I have also included a list of strategies that can be used to effectively assist in overcoming such barriers.

¤　Focusing on a Personal Agenda

When we spend our listening time formulating our next response, we cannot be fully attentive to what the speaker is saying.

¤　Experiencing Information Overload

Too much stimulation or information can make it very difficult to listen with full attention. You should try to focus on the relevant information and the central points that are being conveyed.

¤　Criticizing the Speaker

You should not be distracted by critical evaluations of the speaker. You should make every attempt to focus on what the speaker is saying or the message rather than the messenger.

¤ Getting Distracted by Emotional Noise

All of us naturally react emotionally to certain words, concepts and ideas, and to a myriad of other cues from speakers (including appearance and non-verbal cues). You should make a conscious effort to quiet your own emotional reactions so that you can listen and respond properly.

¤ Getting Distracted by External Noise

Audible noise may be extremely distracting. Some things can be minimized, such as turning down the ringer on your phone and the sounds on your computer while meeting with someone.

¤ Experiencing Physical Difficulty

Feeling physically ill or experiencing pain can make it very difficult to listen effectively. You may wish to communicate that this is not a good time and reschedule the discussion. Otherwise, you may just need to concentrate even more on the task of listening.

Strategies for Overcoming Barriers to Listening

Stop. You should focus on the other person, their thoughts and feelings. Make an attempt to consciously focus on quieting your own internal commentary and step away from your own concerns to think about those of the speaker. Give your full attention to the speaker.

Look. You should pay attention to non-verbal messages, without letting yourself be distracted. Notice body language and non-verbal cues to allow for a richer understanding of the speaker's point. However, avoid getting distracted from the verbal message.

Listen. You should listen for the essence of the speaker's thoughts, details, major ideas and their meanings. Seek an overall understanding of what the speaker is trying to communicate, rather than reacting to the individual words or terms that they use to express themselves.

Be Empathetic. You should try to imagine how you would feel if you were in their circumstances. Be empathetic to the feelings of the speaker, while maintaining a calm center within you. You need not be drawn into all of their problems or issues, as long as you acknowledge what they are experiencing.

Ask Questions. You should use questions to clarify your understanding, as well as to demonstrate interest in what is being said.

Barriers to Accurate Perception

The following are examples of some barriers to you obtaining an accurate perception of someone or a situation. I have also included a list of strategies that can be used to effectively assist in overcoming such barriers.

¤ **Stereotyping and Generalizing**

Be careful not to hold on to preconceptions about people or things. We often have a tendency to see what we want to see, forming an impression from a small amount of information or one experience and assuming that to be highly representative of the whole person or situation.

¤ **Not Investing Time**

Making assumptions and ignoring details or circumstances can lead to misconceptions. When we fail to look in-depth for causes or circumstances, we miss important details and do not allow for the complexity of the situation.

¤ Having a Distorted Focus

Focusing on the negative aspects of a conversation or a situation is a habit common to many of us. Even though we may recognize the positive things, we often give more weight to the negative, allowing one negative comment to overshadow numerous positive ones.

¤ Assuming Similar Interpretations

Not everyone will draw the same conclusions from a given situation or set of information. Everybody interprets things differently. Make sure to check for other people's interpretations and be explicit about your own.

¤ Experiencing Incongruent Cues

As speakers, and as listeners, we are constantly and simultaneously sending cues and receiving them from other people. You should try to be consistent with your verbal cues and your body language. You should refrain from saying one thing and expressing something else through your body language. You should be aware of how your non-verbal communication relates to your spoken words. If someone else seems to be sending a double message -- by saying one thing and expressing something else in their body language -- ask for clarification.

Strategies for Overcoming Barriers to Accurate Perception

Analyze Your Own Perceptions. You should question your perceptions, and think about how they are formed. Check in with others around you regularly and be aware of assumptions that you are making. You can also seek additional information and observations. You may just need to ask people if your perceptions are accurate.

Work on Improving Your Perception. One way to do this is to increase your awareness of barriers to perception and which ones you tend towards. You should check in with yourself regularly. Seek honest, constructive feedback from others regarding their perceptions of you as a means of increasing your self-awareness.

Focus on Others. You should develop your ability to focus on other people and understand them better by trying to gather knowledge about them, listening to them actively, and imagining how you would feel in their situation.

Barriers to Effective Verbal Communication

There are many obvious and not so obvious barriers to verbal communication and these may occur at any stage in the communication process. Barriers may lead to your message becoming distorted. Effective verbal communication involves overcoming these barriers and conveying a clear and concise message. The following are examples of such barriers. I have also included a list of strategies that can be used to effectively assist in overcoming them.

¤ **Lacking Clarity**

You should avoid abstract, overly-formal language, colloquialisms and jargon, which obscure your message more than they serve to impress people.

¤ **Stereotyping Complex Systems or Situations**

Leaders and speakers who make unqualified generalizations undermine their own clarity and leadership. Be careful not to get stuck in the habit of using stereotypes or making generalizations about complex systems or situations. Another form of generalization is "polarization" or creating extremes. Try to be sensitive to the complexities of situations, rather than viewing the world in black and white.

¤ Jumping to Conclusions

Confusing facts with inferences is a common tendency. Do not assume you know the reasons behind events or that certain facts necessarily have certain implications. Make sure you have all the information you can get and then speak clearly about the facts versus the meanings or interpretations you attach to those.

¤ Dysfunctional Responses

Ignoring or not responding to a comment or question quickly undermines effective communication. Likewise, responding with an irrelevant comment -- one that is not connected to the topic at hand -- will quash genuine communication. Interrupting others while they are speaking also creates a poor environment for communication.

¤ Lacking Confidence

Lacking confidence can be a major barrier to effective communication and clarity. Shyness, difficulty being assertive or lack of self-worth can hinder your ability to make your needs and opinions known. Also, a lack of awareness of your own rights and opportunities in a given situation can prevent you from expressing your needs openly.

Strategies for Effective Verbal Communication

Focus on the Issue, Not the Person. You should try not to take everything personally, and similarly, express your own needs and opinions in terms of the job at hand. Solve problems rather than attempt to control others. For example, rather than criticizing a co-worker's personality, express your concerns in terms of how to get the job done more smoothly in the future.

Be Genuine. You should be yourself, authentic, honest and open. Be honest with yourself and focus on working well with the people around you and acting with integrity.

Empathize. Although professional relationships with others entail some boundaries when it comes to interaction with colleagues, it is important to demonstrate sensitivity and to really care about the people you work with. If you do not care about them, it will be difficult for them to care about you when it comes to working together.

Be Flexible. You should allow for other points of view, and be open to other ways of doing things. Diversity brings creativity and innovation.

Value Your Own Experiences. You should be firm about your own rights, desires and needs. Undervaluing yourself encourages others to undervalue you, too. Offer your ideas and expect to be treated well.

Present Yourself as an Equal. Even when you are in a position of authority, focus on what you and the other person each have to offer and to contribute to the job or issue.

Use Affirming Responses. Respond to others in ways that acknowledge their experiences. Thank them for their input. Affirm their right to their feelings, even if you disagree. Ask questions, express positive feeling and provide positive feedback when possible.

The following diagram summarizes the personal goals you should pursue to enable *Clarity* to play a role in helping you maximize your Leadership Advantage.

The Leadership Advantage

Average Level of Clarity	Maximum Level of Clarity
You are aware that there are communication barriers, however you have not taken any actions to identify them.	You have identified your primary barriers to effective listening and communicating.
You address communication barriers when you are faced with them.	You develop specific and actionable strategies to address perceived barriers prior to all major communications.
You address what might appear as inaccurate perceptions doing the "heat of the moment" and hope things work out.	You are aware of the most effective strategies to overcome perception barriers and you deploy them as required.
You depend on your intuition to guide you around communication barriers.	You have developed the skills required to positively navigate through the most common barriers to communication.
	The Leadership Advantage

CHAPTER FOUR

LEADERSHIP AND
PERSISTENCE

"Patience, persistence and perspiration make an unbeatable combination for success."

—Napoleon Hill, *American author in the area of the new thought movement*

We all have exhibited a level of persistence in order to have achieved our current position in life. Persistence is the quality that allows us to continue doing something or trying to do something even though it is difficult or maybe opposed by others.

Persistence is a quality that we, as leaders, should all nurture and view as an advantage that can be utilized in both our professional and personal lives. Your ability to hold on or to get back up after you have been knocked down has been essential for the success you have achieved. As we all know, there will be failures along the way and it is your level and use of this important *Absolute Attribute* that will help you turn failures into stepping stones to future successes.

Calvin Coolidge, 30th United States President, once said *"Nothing in the world can take the place of persistence. Talent will not; nothing is more common than unsuccessful men with talent. Genius will not; unrewarded genius is almost proverb. Education will not; the world is full of educated derelicts. Persistence and determination alone are omnipotent."*

As an *Absolute Attribute, Persistence* allows us to begin, do and finish. Persistence reinforces and strengthens all of the other *Absolute Attributes.* Persistence is essential to being an effective leader as well as achieving your maximum Leadership Advantage.

However, in order to maintain and expand our natural levels of persistence, we all can benefit from some basic techniques which will increase our consciousness and sharpen our awareness of what makes us persistent.

In this chapter, we will briefly overview some of those techniques and highlight how you can leverage your business or organizational approaches by applying these techniques in all aspects of your professional and personal life.

Face Problems Head On

It is not your problems that define you—it is how you react and recover from them. Your problems are not going away unless you do something about them. Facing problems in business and organizational settings tend to be an easier task as compared to your personal life. In these settings, as a leader, you have access to experts (finance, logistics, human resources, legal, etc.) who assist in defining the problem. They also look to you to integrate the facts and realities and to lead them, and the organization, to successful outcomes. In other words, these external resources and organizational roles augment your innate level of persistence. The key to gaining this Leadership Advantage in all aspects of your professional and personal life is approaching every problem not only "head on" but also with a strategy to utilize all of the internal and external expertise you can muster to tackle it. You will greatly benefit from the expanded level of insight, determination and persistence.

Be Passionate about What You Do

Choosing projects that you are passionate about makes being persistent more natural. But, if you go into something half-heartedly or because you feel obliged, the hard times seem harder.

If you continuously get stopped in an area and lack the motivation to continue, you should stop, take a close look and see what is going on. It might be that you are not really inspired about what you are doing or maybe you have just lost sight of the bigger picture of why you are doing what you are doing. In both your professional and personal life, there will be some projects, assignments or tasks that you get to choose and others that you do not get to choose.

Regardless of how the task at hand surfaced, the more passionate you are about getting it done, the more persistence you will be about achieving the desired outcome.

Be Honest with Yourself

Be honest about what you want to achieve, how you want to be perceived when it is accomplished and the obstacles that may prevent you from successfully executing a project, assignment or task. Just as being a fair and honest leader is critical to your long term professional success, being honest with yourself, in all aspects of your life, yields many long term benefits as well. When you are striving to be the best that you can be, honesty has to be at the foundation. Honesty is the bridge to authenticity and self-compassion. Honesty allows you to set realistic goals. It bolsters your courage and unleashes your highest levels of confidence, determination and persistence.

Choose your Battles Wisely

Have you ever found yourself in the middle of a situation or challenge and suddenly come to the realization that you do not really want a particular goal as much as you once thought. You may end up choosing not to be persistent in that endeavor.

The Leadership Advantage

While *Persistence* is an *Absolute Attribute* that seems to always enhance all of the others, there are times when "less is better." If you find yourself in a situation where you are running into a brick wall over and over again and getting no closer to your goal, then persistence is not a good thing. It is vital here is figure out if you have chosen the best path to reach the goal.

Just as in your professional life, challenges in all aspects of your life require a way to weed out what is important to you and reprioritizing. It is important to determine whether the battle you have chosen is worthy of your "dogged persistence."

Remember the Reasons you want to reach your Goal

When you feel your determination begin to waver, remember the reason you want to accomplish your goal. For most of us, the only goals we will succeed in reaching are those that are truly important to us. Keeping the reasons established for reaching a goal prominently in front of you is important to maintaining the level of persistence required to fully achieve the desired outcomes.

The following diagram summarizes the personal goals you should pursue to enable *Persistence* to play a role in helping you maximize your Leadership Advantage.

The Leadership Advantage

Average Level of Persistence	Maximum Level of Persistence
You tend to resist facing most problems head on unless they become unavoidable.	You consciously take all problems head on and utilize all of the expertise you can muster to tackle them.
You are passionate about most of what you do, but sometimes find yourself taking on some tasks half-heartedly.	You are always passionate about what you do in both your professional and personal life.
You are sometimes not honest with yourself and find it difficult to maintain a high level of persistence doing some tasks.	You are always honest with yourself in all aspects of your life. You strive to set realistic goals.
You do not choose your battles wisely and sometimes question if the task is worthy of your persistence.	You choose your battles wisely and persist in all endeavors you undertake.
	The Leadership Advantage

CHAPTER FIVE
LEADERSHIP AND
MOTIVATION

"Of course motivation is not permanent. But then, neither is bathing; but it is something you should do on a regular basis."

—Zig Ziglar, *motivational teacher and trainer*

We all have been motivated by something or someone at multiple-points in our lives and our careers. But do we really know why? More importantly, if the motivator was in a leadership position, was the motivation due to inspiration or unrecognized coercion? A motivator is a person who makes others enthusiastic about doing something. Unfortunately, the enthusiasm could be the results of inspiration or coercion. The latter of which is usually short-lived and creates a new set of issues. An effective leader, on the other hand, is a person who guides or directs others. It is much easier to guide or direct someone who is motivated to follow you. Both good motivators and good leaders have the skills and training required to accomplish the desired outcomes, if they are to be successful.

However, I have found *motivational leadership* to be more of an art form. Good motivational leaders must first understand the art of motivation and how to use their innate motivational skills to implement a model and strategy that work for them as they guide and direct others. Too often many of us tend to believe that leadership skills are synonymous with motivational skills. Although there are some common components, there are also some distinct differences.

As an *Absolute Attribute*, *Motivation* is the ability to uplift and inspire people to perform at their best. However, in order to maximize your Leadership Advantage, you must leverage your motivational skills to motivate yourself to do what is required. Then, you should strive to be the kind of person that makes you the best motivational leader you can be. Both are necessary for maximum performance.

In this chapter we will explore four fundamental but imperative questions regarding motivation and how this broad reaching *Absolute Attribute* can contribute to maximizing your Leadership Advantage. They are:

¤ What is Motivation?
¤ What are the Components of Motivation?
¤ What You can do to Strengthen Your Motivation? and
¤ How to Lead and Motivate Yourself?

What is Motivation?

Motivation is defined as the process that initiates, guides and maintains goal-oriented behaviors. Motivation is what causes us to act, whether it is getting a glass of water to reduce thirst or reading a book to gain knowledge.

Motivation involves the biological, emotional, social, and cognitive forces that activate behavior. In everyday usage, the term motivation is frequently used to describe why a person does something. For example, you might say that a student is so motivated to get into a leadership program that she spends every night studying.

The term motivation refers to factors that activate, direct and sustain goal-directed behavior. Motives are the "whys" of behavior --- the needs or wants that drive behavior and explain what we do. We do not actually observe a motive. Rather, we infer that one exists based on the behavior we observe.

Psychologists have proposed a number of different theories of motivation, including drive theory, instinct theory, and humanistic theory. You should spend more time reviewing these intriguing theories to gain a better sense of their depth.

What are the Components of Motivation?

Anyone who has ever had a goal (like wanting to lose ten pounds or wanting to run a marathon) probably immediately realizes that simply having the desire to accomplish something is not enough. Achieving such a goal requires the ability to persist through obstacles and the endurance to keep going in spite of difficulties.

The two main components to motivation are *activation* and *persistence.*

Activation involves the decision to initiate a behavior, such as enrolling in a leadership class.

Persistence is the continued effort toward a goal even though obstacles may exist, such as taking more leadership courses in order to earn a degree although it requires a significant investment of time, energy, and resources.

There are two types of motivation, *extrinsic* and *intrinsic.* Here is a quick explanation and discussion on each of the two types.

Extrinsic Motivation

A person is extrinsically motivated when the primary source of motivation is to attain a tangible outcome such as a reward, or to avoid a negative consequence such as a punishment. In a work setting, people are extrinsically motivated if the principal reason for their effort at work is pay, positive performance reviews, opportunities for advancement and bonuses. Similarly, people are also extrinsically motivated if the principal reason for the effort at work is to avoid reprimands, poor performance reviews, poor assignments and dismissals. Notice that with extrinsic motivation, the source of the motivation is external to the task itself. The tangible outcome we seek, such as a pay raise, is invariably administered (or controlled) by someone else.

Intrinsic Motivation

The second type of motivation is intrinsic motivation. People are intrinsically motivated when the principal reason for their effort at work is that they find the work itself exciting, challenging, fulfilling, interesting and energizing. Furthermore, they get feelings of pride, feelings of achievement and feelings of accomplishment when working on these tasks.

What You can do to Strengthen your Motivation?

Motivation is like a muscle. You need to practice strengthening it through a regular routine. Here are some documented ways for increasing, maintaining and strengthening your motivation.

¤ **Set Small, Measurable Goals**.

If you have a major goal, it would be a good idea if you split it into several minor goals with each small goal leading to your major goal. This way you will find it easier to motivate yourself. You will also not feel overwhelmed by the size of your goal and the things you have to do. This will also help you feel that the goal is more feasible and easier to accomplish.

¤ **Develop a Mantra.**

A mantra is a verbal statement that reinforces a positive mindset. A mantra can be extremely helpful when it comes to keeping your motivation up and your spirits high. Come up with a statement that really resonates with you.

¤ **Face your Fears.**

If pessimism is an obstacle to motivation, fear is the entire obstacle course. Fears come in all shapes and sizes. No matter what the fear, fear is one of the biggest reasons why people give up on their goals and dreams. What many fail to realize, however, is that on the other side of fear is confidence. While scary, facing your fears gives you a great sense of accomplishment and allows you to broaden your horizons. If you can tackle one small fear, what is to stop you from tackling a larger one?

¤ **Become a Good Mental Debater.**

The journey to obtaining a goal has its peaks and valleys. In order to keep your motivation up, it is important to learn optimism. Believe it or not, optimism is a learned mental state. The first step to learning optimism is to acknowledge the moments when you are being pessimistic. Once they have been acknowledged, you have the power to debate pessimism away. Practice using a positive frame of mind to talk away all of your doubts and negative thoughts.

¤ **Visualize your Goals.**

Goals can change and evolve day to day. However, if you create a great visualization of what it will be like once a specific goal is achieved, it can provide a motivating feeling of happiness and joy.

¤ **Keep your Eye on the Finish Line.**

Understand that finishing what you start is important. Hammer into your mind that whatever you start you must finish. Develop the habit of going to the finish line.

¤ **Constantly Affirm your Success.**

Affirmations are positive declarations, statements or judgments. Affirmations can be a powerful source of strength and focus. They can be repeated to yourself out loud or silently in your head to help affirm to yourself that you can, and will succeed.

How to Lead and Motivate Yourself?

As leaders, we know that one of our major responsibilities is to keep our team motivated. To do so, we must constantly remind our people of the organization's vision, hold them accountable to targets and goals, mentor them and support them in their work. But, how does the one who motivates others every day stay motivated as well?

When it comes to leaders, motivation is really about engagement. How engaged are you in your work? How committed are you to the results you are supposed to be getting? Are you pushing forward with a sense of purpose and drive, or are you simply going through motions? To be your best and to obtain maximum Leadership Advantage, you need to give serious thought to what makes you flourish and succeed.

When you are motivated, you are a wholehearted participant in your own life. You know what is important to you and you use it as a guide. You feel confident, energized and engaged. However, when you are de-motivated, you "lose your edge." Your energy goes down. Your stress goes up. You may even feel guilty and resentful. You might even become bored and actually tune-out.

Whatever way a lack of motivation hits you, one thing is for sure – it is not a fun place to be.

Whether you feel your motivation waning or you want to keep your current high level of motivation on a roll, the following suggestions will help you stay at your best.

¤ **Stay Connected to What you are Doing.**

It is one thing to do the work you are paid to do. It is another thing to be fulfilled by the work you do. If you are strictly doing your job for the money, or the title, or the company car, you could find that over time it is harder and harder to actually do the job.

However, if you are connected to what you do and you are connected to what excites you, you will feel motivated to keep going because you will be achieving a bigger purpose for yourself.

The vital thing is to know your values. Your values are the principles, standards and qualities that guide you. To uncover your values you may have to recall a time in your life when everything was "just right." You could choose something from your personal life or your work. You might revisit a moment, a particular event, or a whole phase of your life. Once you have allowed yourself some time to explore the memory, ask yourself what it was about that memory that made it so memorable, so significant, and so right. What made it a peak experience? Write down any ideas that come to mind – words, phrases, images and symbols. When you have finished with your notes, circle the words that meet the definition of values, including principles, standards and qualities. There is no right or wrong during this process. Simply use your own words and your gut to tell you what your values are.

¤ **Know What it Takes to Get Better.**

Motivation comes from constant learning on how to be better. Therefore, you should always be asking yourself, "What am I trying to achieve?" and "What do I need to learn to reach my goal?" You should realize that this is not about taking a workshop or reading a book. It is about challenging yourself to take on something new and to stretch yourself into a new level of results.

The fact is that when you practice learning as an element of motivational leadership, you too will stay motivated and you get better results for yourself, for your Associates and for your work. By learning, you empower yourself to have, do and be whatever you choose. And with empowerment comes confidence. You do not second-guess yourself or worry you will fail, because you know if you get it wrong, you will be able to figure out how to get it right.

⋈ **Find the Right Support System.**

When you are a leader, all of the people below you must lean on you. You guide them, support them and tell them what to do.

However, when you are on top, you do not have anyone above you to lean on. That is when you need to look outside of your organization, your role or even your industry for the people who can cheer you on, mentor you and help you be your best. To do so, look for people whose style you like. They should be people who inspire you by the way they lead and the results they get. Seek out people who resonate with you and who seem to mirror parts of yourself. You should connect with them to see what is possible for you as a leader. You should learn how you can become more with the help of others who have already done what you want to do. The more carefully you build your support team, the more powerful it will be. You should not ask people to mentor you because you like them. You should make them a part of your team because they enhance you. The people on your support team can help you stay motivated. They can expand you by giving you access to what you do not know. Remember, it does not have to be lonely at the top.

¤ **Maintain a Sense of Balance.**

While maintaining a work and life balance is not a way to stay motivated, it is a way to keep from becoming demotivated. When you are serving everyone else, you have to remember to fill your own tank. Remember that being an effective and motivated leader should not come at the expense of quality of life and your quality of life should not come at the expense of business results. Work and life should be able to co-exist, happily and successfully.

The key is to define what that balance looks like for you. If you are a senior leader, balance may not look very traditional. It might not be a nine-to-five job, Monday through Friday, with holidays and weekends off. You need to understand what works for you and what fulfills you in your personal life. What helps you restore your energy and find that sense of peace, rest and renewal? Depending on your lifestyle and personal preferences, that could be taking a morning job, sleeping in on days off, reading a fiction book or spending time with family. Even if you cannot carve out chunks of time, at least create some mental space where you can relax, turn off distractions and let yourself go.

The following diagram summarizes the personal goals you should pursue to enable *Motivation* to play a role in helping you maximize your Leadership Advantage.

Average Level of Motivation	Maximum Level of Motivation
You sometimes find yourself not connected to what you are doing and find it difficult to stay alert, focused and motivated.	You make sure you stay connected to what you're doing, it excites you and you feel motivated to keep going.
You are occasionally searching for what you need to do to get better and many times settle for mediocre performances.	You know what it takes to get better and challenge yourself by stretching for better results.
You find yourself on the top and don't have anyone above you to lean on. You struggle to find the right support system.	You seek out and connect with people who resonate with you to maintain peak levels of motivation.
You often feel like you are always serving everyone else and forget to fill your own tank.	You maintain a good sense of work/life balance as a way to keep from becoming demotivated.
	The Leadership Advantage

"Desire is the key to motivation, but its determination and commitment to an unrelenting pursuit of your goal — a commitment to excellence — that will enable you to attain the success you seek."

–Mario Andretti, Italian American world champion racing driver

CHAPTER SIX

LEADERSHIP AND
UNSELFISHNESS

"A wise unselfishness is not a surrender of yourself to the wishes of anyone, but only to the best discoverable course of action."

— David Seabury, *American psychologist, author, ad lecturer*

The Leadership Advantage

We all have learned that being an effective team member requires a degree of compromise and unselfishness. Well, it is even more important to understand the role that unselfishness and compromise play for us as leaders and in our ability to maximize our Leadership Advantage.

Unselfishness is a very popular ideal, one that has been honored throughout recorded history. Unselfishness is commonly defined as having or showing more concern for other people than for yourself---i.e. not being selfish. However, from an organizational and leadership perspective, my experience has taught me to think of unselfishness as much more than "having or showing more concern for other people." In terms of your Leadership Advantage, unselfishness is a key leadership trait that is both noticed and valued by others.

Professionally, a competent leader who is unselfish and who has the best interests of the organization at heart has followers who duly recognize this attribute. As such, they will offer a level of support that could provide significant advantage in difficult times. Personally, as you continue your quest to develop your skills and to become the best you, unselfishness will increase your chances by attracting and maintaining the strong support of others.

Now, my experience has taught me that unselfishness is not only essential to setting the foundation of a good leader but it is also a skill that must be developed. Your willingness and ability to sacrifice for others and put your own personal needs and desires second requires focus. It also requires sensitivity and the understanding of another trait that is often mis-understood --- compromise.

Webster's New World Dictionary defines compromise as primarily "a settlement in which each side gives up some demands or makes concessions." Unfortunately the word compromise has become a judgmental term, something similar to selling out. In reality, compromise means working things out, or as Webster's says in a secondary meaning, "an adjustment of opposing principles." As such, compromise is essential to getting things done, not only in your professional life but also in your personal life. It can mean the difference between failure and success. Compromise is essential to any negotiations process.

The Leadership Advantage

As an *Absolute Attribute*, *Unselfishness* is anchored by compromise. An unselfish leader's openness and generosity is very likely to accrue significant benefits in both a personal and professional sense. A selfish leader who grabs all the credit and deflects all the blame will, at some point, find the world a very lonely place.

In this chapter we will first briefly explore three perspectives that you should embrace while leading yourself, your organization or your family through compromise. They are:

- ¤ Positive Intent makes the Process of Compromise Productive;
- ¤ Collaboration is a Way to Achieve Effective Compromise; and
- ¤ Synergy is a Positive Result of Great Compromise.

Then, we will explore some examples which can help to answer two common questions that many experienced leaders ask themselves --- What is it that "unselfish leaders" do and how do they behave?

Three Perspectives to use in Leading through Compromise

Leading is not kicking the can down the road. Those who take full advantage of their Leadership Advantage pick the can up, understand its' contents and determine how, whatever is inside, can be resolved or refreshed to improve their personal or organizational performance as well as the lives of the people involved. Unselfishness and compromise are valuable tools in your arsenal.

Here are three perspectives that you should embrace while leading through compromise.

1. Positive Intent makes the Process of Compromise Productive

If you go into a situation requiring compromise, then go into it with a positive attitude on how to bring people together and focus on developing a real, better solution. Others in the room will be different than you and will have different values and ideas on how to solve an issue. Listen positively. Engage with the intent to solve. Keep focused on the larger objective and what it requires.

2. Collaboration is a Way to Achieve Effective Compromise

Collaboration is working together, leveraging another's strengths and finding ways to create a better solution. Ideas enhanced and supported by a larger group will gain in strength and momentum. Adopt a collaborative mindset as you approach to the problem, the challenge, the choice and the decision.

3. Synergy is a Positive Result of Great Compromise

Rather than focusing on a minimal compromise or just continued disagreement, focus on synergy. Given the higher goal and the different ideas, how can they be brought together in the best way and create a better-than-incremental solution? In other words, go beyond just compromise and create a better opportunity for success together.

What is it that Unselfish Leaders Do and How do they Behave?

The process of leading others is a human endeavor, not a science that can be quantified and categorized to fit into a neat set of instructions for success. Every individual is gifted with different levels of ability and capability to lead others. However, the resulting success or failure is not solely based on those abilities. Here are some examples of what many leaders do and how they behave when they successfully deploy an effective and meaningful degree of unselfishness and compromise.

¤ **Shares the Credit.**

Associates, who are recognized for their winning efforts, whether in the foreground or background, feel a sense of pride in and loyalty to their company and their leader. Since everyone wants to work for such a leader, a deep pool of talent very often ensues.

¤ **Takes the Time to Teach.**

Teaching is a critical role for a leader. The unselfish leader finds the time to teach Associates not only about business processes and results, company goals and objectives, but also about ethical and behavioral standards that are important to the organization and the leader.

¤ **Accepts Responsibility for their Associates' Shortcomings.**

An unselfish leader is not quick to blame others or make excuses when Associates inevitably mess up. The leader first finds the fix to the problem, followed with coaching and counseling, and then looks for ways to improve the process and the training. Learning from mistakes is critical to continuous improvement. Giving Associates room to make mistakes and allow them to learn and gain confidence as a result, is an unselfish and courageous act for a leader.

94

¤ **Accepts and Shares the Ideas and Input of Others.**

An unselfish leader is open to new ideas and concepts, and from a variety of sources. So very often the Associates actually doing the work have the best ideas on how a particular process can be improved. Let others be the experts. Build the bench strength by developing technical and leadership skills in your Associates. Help others to succeed and reinforce the "unselfish" trait.

The following diagram summarizes the personal goals you should pursue to enable *Unselfishness* to play a role in helping you maximize your Leadership Advantage.

The Leadership Advantage

Average Level of Unselfishness	Maximum Level of Unselfishness
You feel that you can more than adequately respond to any situation that requires you to be less selfish and to compromise.	You work on developing the skills to be unselfish and to compromise as required to achieve the best outcomes.
You approach most situations with the solution that you feel is best and a strategy to persuade the team.	You approach all situations requiring compromise, with a positive attitude and focus on developing the best solution.
You only recognize Associates for outstanding effort and only to the degree to which they deserve recognition.	You always recognize efforts of Associates and ensure that they share in all rewards to the greatest extent possible.
You are usually as unselfish as you need to be and generally only compromise if it is the last resort.	You know that unselfishness is anchored by compromise and you work to improve your skills in both areas.
	The Leadership Advantage

CHAPTER SEVEN

LEADERSHIP AND
DELIBERATION

"Deliberation, n.: The act of examining one's bread to determine which side it is buttered on."

—*Ambrose Bierce,*
American editorialist, journalist,
short story writer

W e all have some ability to be thoughtful and deliberate. But how can we prevent too much deliberation or the lack of deliberation from negatively impacting our ability to reach our goals. Well, in terms of maximizing your *Leadership Advantage*, deliberation is something that cannot be measured by too much or too little. Deliberation is a combination of a process and an art. In the broadest terms, leadership in itself is the art of leading others to deliberately create a result that wouldn't have happened otherwise.

The noun deliberation comes from the Latin word "deliberare", meaning "weigh," or "consider well." When you guide your team through all of the possible solutions to a problem, you are in deliberation. Deliberation is a carefully thought-out process of making a decision, setting a course of action and following through with concise execution.

As one of the *Ten Absolute Attributes* associated with your Leadership Advantage, *Deliberation* is an artful process which delivers results and satisfaction as well as a sense of involvement.

When we deliberate with others, the deliberation process is collaborative and involves more than just one person's experience, needs and perspective. At its best, deliberation requires a commitment on the part of all who enter into the process to listen to the perspectives and the knowledge of all who are participating and to try to learn from one another.

In this chapter we will explore the following aspects of the process of deliberation and how you, as a leader, can leverage this attribute to generate even better outcomes:

- ¤ How is Deliberation Different from Debate?

- ¤ Why is it Important to Know How to Deliberate?

- ¤ What are some Basic Guidelines for Deliberation? and

- ¤ What are some Tips for Facilitating the Deliberation Process?

How is Deliberation Different from Debate?

Deliberation is not foreign. In some form, it is very familiar to all of us. When we have to make an important decision, we deliberate. We consider the merits of a range of alternatives and weigh the advantages as well as the tradeoffs of each. After thinking the issue through, we try to make the best possible choice. We then select the one that best addresses our particular needs. It may not be perfect, but it is informed by all of the information that we can bring to the decision at that time.

In a deliberation, everyone expects to end up in a different place as a result of the discussion and decisions made. You contribute your knowledge and perspective to the whole, listening to and building on the contributions of others. By engaging in shared ideas, everyone grows in knowledge, skills and understanding.

Deliberation is not a debate. In a debate, you hold onto your position with the intent that you will "win" the argument and everyone else will end up in a different place. Debate is a competitive process in which there are winners and losers. Ideas are not built. Ideas are contested. Deliberation is a more collaborative process. The aim of deliberation is to share perspectives and knowledge and to build ideas --- not to defend them.

Why is it Important to Know How to Deliberate?

As professionals, we all know why debate skills are useful. We use these skills when we want to persuade another of the merits of our ideas. But what if our ideas are not fully formed? What if the issue is complex and involves multiple interests? How do you generate new approaches that address multiple needs?

This calls for careful listening and being open to the knowledge and the views of others. It requires building new ideas and new approaches together. This is deliberation. Deliberation is a cornerstone of true leadership and for maximizing your Leadership Advantage. Professionally, learning and enhancing deliberative skills will increase your capacity to main better decisions, build stronger teams and develop the skills of your entire organization. In your personal life, these skills and the mastery of the art will allow you to better connect with others and to form stronger relationships.

What are some Basic Guidelines for Deliberation?

Here are seven basic guidelines that can aid in maintaining a high level of consciousness when you engage in the deliberation process in almost any setting.

1. Always speak your mind freely, but do not monopolize the conversation. You should enter the deliberation with some knowledge of all the others that are involved and cognizant of the personalities and pressures.

2. Listen carefully to others. Do not fall in the trap of gathering your thoughts while someone else is speaking. You may miss some the key points that are being made. You should try to really understand what others are saying and respond to them fully. This is especially important when their ideas are different from your own.

3. You should avoid building your own argument in your head while others are talking. If you are afraid you will forget a point, write it down.

4. Paraphrase others points of view to help confirm the understanding of their points and positions.

5. Be open to changing your mind. This will help you really listen to others' points of view.

6. When disagreement occurs, do not personalize it. Keep talking and explore the disagreement. Look for the common concerns beneath the surface.

7. Be careful not to discredit another person's point of view. Remember that, although you are trying to listen to and build on each other's ideas, it does not mean that everyone has to end up in the same place.

What are some Tips for Facilitating the Deliberation Process?

As a leader tasked with the facilitation of a deliberative session, you are responsible for maintaining the flow of the discussion, encouraging opportunities for participation, and assuring a respectful and open environment that allows for the meaningful discussion and exchange of views that take place in a successful deliberative process. Here are some proven tips that will aid in both facilitating the deliberation process as well as leveraging some inherit leadership skills.

- ¤ Listen actively.

- ¤ Engage everyone in the discussion.

- ¤ Do not speak after each comment or answer every question.

- ¤ Encourage participants to talk to each other, not to you.

- ¤ Help the group to look at the issues from many different points of view.

- ¤ If one or more perspectives are not getting a fair hearing, ask if someone in the group can make a case for that view.

- ¤ Help the group to identify and summarize commonality as the discussion move forward.

However, you should not force it. You do not want to unwittingly silence more restrained contributors.

The following diagram summarizes the personal goals you should pursue to enable *Deliberation* to play a role in helping you maximize your Leadership Advantage.

Average Level of Deliberation	Maximum Level of Deliberation
You enter deliberation only when you are not able to sell your idea or position outright without getting others involved.	You see deliberation as a process which can aid in making the best possible choice.
You prepare for a deliberation as you would a debate or any competitive process in which there are winners and losers.	You consider a strategic range of alternatives and weigh the advantages as well as the tradeoffs of each when you deliberate.
You strategically guard your thoughts and points-of-view until the best time to score points and move the discussion in your favor.	You always speak your mind freely, but don't monopolize the conversation while in deliberation sessions.
You understand that the aim of deliberation is to share and listen to other perspectives but find it a waste of time when you feel that you have the right answer.	You know that the aim of deliberation is to share perspectives and to build ideas, not to defend them.
	The Leadership Advantage

"Success is not final, failure is not fatal: it is the courage to continue that counts."

— Winston S. Churchill,
British statesman

CHAPTER EIGHT

LEADERSHIP AND
COURAGE

"Courage is the most important of all the virtues because without courage, you can't practice any other virtue consistently."
— Maya Angelou, *American poet, memoirist, actress*

We all have some mental or moral strength to persevere and withstand danger, fear, or difficulty. However, because courage is required in almost every basic human activity or endeavor, how do we ration our courageousness consistent with results that can be expected?

Certainly, courage in our daily lives can sometimes be a matter of life and death. In some occupations like being a police officer or firefighter you are expected to routinely take courageous actions. The courage in these occupations seems to be instinctive and reactionary. However, there have been many studies on human behavior in organizations and they all seem to indicate that courage in business seldom operates like this. Leaders who act courageously, whether on behalf of society, their companies, their colleagues or their own career rarely do it impulsively. Nor does it emerge from nowhere.

In business, courageous action is really a special kind of calculated risk taking. As we discussed in the previous chapter, those of us who become good leaders have a greater than average willingness to make bold moves, but they strengthen their chances of success—and avoid career suicide—through careful deliberation and preparation.

Business courage is not so much a visionary leader's inborn characteristic as it is a skill acquired through decision-making processes that improve with practice. In other words, to maximize your Leadership Advantage you must teach yourself how to make high-risk decisions. Much of the ability to be a truly courageous leader is learned and leverages the skills associated with the other nine *Absolute Attributes*. Remember, courageous leadership blossoms over time.

As Mark Twain once wrote, "Courage is not the absence of fear, but its mastery." Mastering the concept of courageous leadership and taking intelligent risks requires an understanding of what I call "*Calculated Risk and Reward.*"

Calculated Risk and Reward is a straight-forward approach of making leadership success more likely while avoiding impulsive, unproductive or irrational behavior. In business, as in life, taking positive, calculated risks is sometimes absolutely necessary in order to achieve an elusive goal or the next level of performance. As with any risk, there is always something at stake. In most instances, when it comes to leadership decisions, you stand to lose money, time, respect and your reputation. Which are also the very same things you stand to gain. The rewards of having an appropriate level of disciplined courage and taking risks can enrich your business, your career and your life.

In this chapter we will briefly discuss the following six discrete steps that make up the *Calculated Risk and Reward* approach to taking courageous leadership actions.

- ¤ Setting Primary and Secondary Goals
- ¤ Determining the Importance of Achieving Your Goals
- ¤ Tipping the Power Balance in Your Favor
- ¤ Weighing Risks against Rewards
- ¤ Selecting the Proper Time for Action
- ¤ Developing Contingency Plans

1. Setting Primary and Secondary Goals

The first step of the Calculated Risk and Reward approach is for you to answer these questions:

- What will success look like? Is it realistically obtainable?

- If my primary goal is organizational, does it defend or advance my company's or team's principles and values?

- If my primary goal is personal, does it derive solely from my career ambitions or also from a desire for my organization's or even society's greater good?
- If I cannot meet my primary goal, what is my secondary goal?

Whether primary or secondary, your goals should be reasonably within reach and not pie-in-the-sky ambitions.

A primary goal that serves the organization might be either to rescue a good Associate or to prevent the senior manager from acting on defective information. A secondary organizational goal might be to apprise a senior manager of internal "people challenges" that are hidden deep in the organization.

A primary goal that serves you personally might be to receive some behind-the-scenes credit for helping the Associate. A secondary personal goal might be to feel that you did something for the greater good.

2. Determining the Importance of Achieving Your Goals

The second step of the Calculated Risk and Reward approach addresses these questions:

- Just how important is it that you achieve your goal or goals?

- If you do not do something about the current state of affairs, will your organization suffer?
- Will your career be derailed?
- Will you be able to look at yourself in the mirror? Does the situation call for immediate, high-profile action or something more nuanced and less risky?

Remember, courageous leadership is not about squandering political capital on low-priority issues.

To distinguish such squandering from constructive risk, you should assign importance at three levels. On the *lowest rung* are issues about which you do not feel strongly, though you may prefer a particular outcome and may address in a low-risk situation. *Middle-rung* issues are those about which your opinion is strong but does not involve higher values. That is, your feelings may change based on new information. At the *top of the ladder* are "fight-worthy" issues. Fight-worthy issues are those that rest on morals or values for which you are willing to take a stand and fight.

3. Tipping the Power Balance in Your Favor

Sometimes, even as seasoned professionals, we often assume that power in our organization is a simple matter of position on the organization chart. In attempting to please more senior leaders, we may choose never to take a stand. But in reality, even those in top management give power to anyone on whom they are dependent—whether for respect, advice, friendship, appreciation or network affiliations.

Seen this way, organizational power is something over which we really do have considerable control. By establishing relationships with and influencing those around you, for example, you gain sway over people who otherwise hold sway over you. This gives you a broader base from which to make bold moves.

4. Weighing Risks Against Rewards

This step of the Calculated Risk and Reward approach focuses on trade-offs and can present these questions:

- Who stands to win?
- Who stands to lose?
- What are the chances that your reputation will be tarnished beyond repair if you go forward?
- Will you lose respect or your job? or cause others to lose theirs?
- Delay your opportunity for promotion?

Other trade-offs deal with the quality of the action and the strategy involved. Are your goals better served if you act in a direct and forceful way or if you take an indirect approach?

5. Selecting the Proper Time for Action

Desmond Tutu, the South African social rights activist and retired Anglican bishop, once described great leaders as having an uncanny sense of timing. "The real leader," he writes, knows "when to make concessions, when to compromise, when to employ the art of losing the battle in order to win the war."

It can be argued that when someone is confronted by a situation that requires courage, the question of timing should be irrelevant. Being in leadership roles sometimes move us to assume that in "fight-worthy" situations, when much is at stake and emotions are running high, brave people do not hesitate to act. This may be true in emergency situations, but a single-minded rush to action in business is usually foolish.

Although emotion is always in the mix, and may even be an asset when making a courageous leadership move, the following questions can help in logically calculating whether the time is right:

• Why am I pursuing this now?

• Am I contemplating a considered action or an impulsive one?

- How long would it take to become better prepared? Is that too long?

- What are the pros and cons of waiting a day, two days, a week or more?

- What are the political obstacles? Can these be either removed or reduced in the near future?

- Can I take steps now that will create a foundation for a courageous move later?

- Am I emotionally and mentally prepared to take this risk?

- Do I have the expertise, communication skills, track record, and credibility to make this work?

Spending too much time on any or all of these questions, of course, can lead you into Hamlet's trap, and the opportunity for courage may pass you by.

At the same time, too little consideration may result in an overly hasty leap. It is important to remember that courageous action in business is for the most part deliberative. Real emergencies are rare. Time may well be on your side. Before you make your move, it is critical to marshal sufficient support, information or evidence to improve your odds of success.

6. Developing Contingency Plans

In general, contingency planning is really about resourcefulness. Leaders who take bold risks and succeed are versatile thinkers; they ready themselves with alternative routes. Courageous leaders prepare themselves for any eventuality, including worst-case scenarios.

In the end, courage in business, as in life, rests on priorities that serve a personal, an organizational, or a societal philosophy. When this philosophy is bolstered by clear, obtainable primary and secondary goals; an evaluation of their importance; a favorable power base; a careful assessment of risks versus benefits; appropriate timing; and well-developed contingency plans --- you are better empowered to make bold moves that serve your organization, your career and your own sense of personal worth.

The following diagram summarizes the personal goals you should pursue to enable *Courage* to play a role in helping you maximize your Leadership Advantage.

The Leadership Advantage

Average Level of Courage	Maximum Level of Courage
You think through each issue which requires risky leadership actions but do not take the time to consider both primary and secondary options.	You always set primary and secondary goals in your approach to taking potentially risky leadership actions.
You usually sense situations which require strong leadership action, react accordingly and hope the action is appropriate.	You always determine if the situation calls for immediate, high-profile action or something more nuanced and less risky.
You sometimes consider available trade-offs before taking risky leadership actions but normally depend on your "gut-feelings."	You always weigh risks against rewards and consider available trade-offs before taking risky leadership actions.
You tend to act quickly and take risky actions without considering the timeliness when emotions are in the mix.	You value the need for an uncanny sense of timing when making a courageous leadership move.
	The Leadership Advantage

118

CHAPTER NINE

LEADERSHIP AND
RESPECT

"Respect was invented to cover the empty place where love should be."

— Leo Tolstoy, *Russian novelist, short story writer, essayist, playwright and philosopher*

The Leadership Advantage

We all desire to be respected and we understand its value in getting things done through others. But, are we capable of consistently giving the proper level of respect to situations and circumstances as well as to individuals?

The 21st century workplace has evolved and has become more trustworthy, transparent, ethical, collaborative and mindful of its team members.

Today's leaders must be equally diligent to earn respect from their Associates and their colleagues. Being the leader does not mean that you have earned respect. Too many of us take our titles and authority for granted. Some of us believe that we are owed or command some level of respect just because of where we are positioned on the organizational chart. Today's workplace is highly influenced by millennials and embedded with people that have trouble trusting others, in general. They require proof of performance before respect is earned. Thus, as 21st century leaders, we must reset

121

our state of mind and become more responsible with our actions and accountable for the effect our influence has on our teams and the organization as a whole.

As one of the Ten *Absolute Attribute*s associated with maximizing your Leadership Advantage, *Respect* is more than just a word. The context of this attribute challenges us to consider what it truly means and what it distinguishes for us. This can make a significant difference in how we observe ourselves, others and our organization. Conventional wisdom considers "respect" to be a kind of feeling or a judgment of a person's "worthiness". However, respect can also be a declaration on the part of the person who is respecting another. If we take this to be the case, then respect is something else altogether.

In this chapter, we will explore the following aspects of Leadership and Respect;

- ¤ What is Respect?
- ¤ What is Respectful Leadership? and
- ¤ How to Leverage the Five Fundamental Pillars of Leadership to Earn the Respect of your Team?

What is Respect?

Respect is one of the values that we hear talked about a lot in organizations. Respect is a word that always evokes a positive conversation. The challenge has been that most leaders rarely think about or understand what it means to respect someone, to create a culture of respect among people or, for that matter, what it means to be respected. Most of us believe that respect is an important value and that it is good. We do not normally think of respect as an action but as a feeling or judgment about other people.

Whether respect is declared or whether it occurs as a judgment, it is an expression of the way the person who is respecting, or not respecting, sees themselves and others. Respect is in the eye of the beholder and is not a function of the behaviors or the attributes of those with whom we are interacting.

Furthermore, many of us propose that to understand respect as an empowering concept, it must also be universal. If respect is a judgment, it becomes a tool of the ego and actually a source of separation and conflict between human beings. The alternative is to understand that respect is an action, a declaration and a commitment on our part of who another person *is* --- separate and apart from whatever judgments we might have of his or her behavior.

If we say we respect someone, we are "looking" at the other person in a particular way — usually suggesting we are open to listen and honor each other's views even if we disagree. If we say we do not respect someone, we are generally "closed" to certain possibilities and conversations with them.

Likewise, if we have "self-respect" we are generally in a healthy internal conversation with ourselves. If we do not respect ourselves, we will typically be stuck in all sorts of unproductive and unsatisfying "self-talk". If we say that something is possible to someone we respect, we will more than likely have a productive and satisfying dialogue. If we do not respect them then we will more than likely be closed, not listen or in some cases disregard and dismiss them and their views outright.

What is Respectful Leadership?

The term, *Respectful Leadership* is a complex one. It has a variety of meanings depending on the context in which it is used. However, respected leaders are most often defined as leaders who consult with their subordinates, respect their expertise and their value to the organization. Respected leaders seem to be able to finds out how they want to be treated and what they consider is respectful to them. They send out a powerful message that actively encourages both self-respect as well as respect for others.

Here are some suggestions that could help you move in the direction of being viewed as a respectful leader.

¤ **Take a Top Down Approach.**

Most good leaders encourage Associates to respect both themselves and others. However, many of these leaders often fail to perceive that respect starts at the top. The way to create a more respectful workplace is to make respect a centerpiece of your leadership approach.

¤ **Encourage Civility.**

Bad manners and questionable behavior should not be viewed as acceptable in a professional workplace. Respectful leadership promotes workplace civility and prepares Associates with conflict resolution skills and processes.

¤ **Emphasize Communication.**

Respectful leaders are great communicators. One of the keys to creating an atmosphere of respect in any business or organization is to include your Associates in your decision-making processes to the fullest extent possible. Although it should always be clear that you are the final decision maker, you will gain the respect of your team if you listen to their input and communicate the rationale behind your decisions.

¤ **Create Partnerships with Team Members.**

Inclusion and collaboration are critical features of respectful leadership. If you treat your team members simply as Associates, you will never gain their full respect. However, if you treat them like valuable partners in executing your organization's mission, they will reward you with their trust, loyalty, and respect.

¤ **Recognize Employee Contributions.**

It is difficult to respect a leader that takes all of the credit for the organization's successes. Respectful leaders recognize the contributions their team members make to their success.

Five Fundamental Pillars of Leadership to Earn the Respect of your Team

To help you achieve sustainable success as a leader who puts people first, here are five ways to earn the respect of your team.

The Leadership Advantage

1. Maintain Consistently Strong Work Ethic and Set Standards

Actions are stronger than words, and this is personified by the respected leader. Great leaders rebuff false promises and people that create lots of unnecessary noise to get attention. There are many leaders that play the role on the outside, but have very little substance on the inside. Respected leaders are those who consistently prove through their work ethic that they are reliable and trustworthy on the inside and out.

These leaders set the tone and are great role models. The tangible and measureable results of their consistent work ethic influence new best practices and cultivate innovation. Ultimately, their leadership defines the performance culture for the organization. They set the standard and leave behind a permanent impact.

2. Do Not be Afraid to Take Risks and Admit Wrong Doing

Respected leaders are those who are not afraid to take risks. They are bold enough to change the conversation and seamlessly challenge the status quo for the betterment of the organization and their competitive advantage. They can anticipate when a paradigm shift is in order and are courageous enough to act on it.

The other side of this admirable trait is the ability to admit wrong doing. Respected leaders do not hesitate to make the most difficult decisions and will put themselves out on the frontline to lead by example. When it is appropriate, they gravitate towards what many view as a "leap of faith" and willingly accept the challenge – knowing very well that the odds may not be in their favor given the personalities and inherent obstacles that surround them.

3. Sponsor High-Potential Associates

Respected leaders think about making others better. They are mindful of those that give one hundred percent of themselves toward their responsibilities. Respected leaders find ways to discover the best in people and enable their full potential. When they detect high-potential talent they impart upon them their wisdom and provide a path for long-term success.

Leaders that "sponsor" their Associates put their own reputation at risk for the betterment of the individuals they are serving. This is an admirable quality and one that is highly respected among a leader's peers.

4. Present a Powerful Executive Presence

A mentioned in the earlier chapters, the most respected leaders are the most authentic people. Their executive presence is genuine and true. They make those around them feel that they matter and they welcome constructive dialogue regardless of hierarchy or rank.

Respected leaders trust themselves enough to live their personal brand and serve as powerful role models to others. Their presence creates long-lasting impact that leaves a positive mark on the organization and the people they serve. Respected leaders are passionate, impact-driven people. Their presence is felt when they walk into the room. Their reputation and their track-record precede them.

5. Give Credit to your Team and Reward Performance

Too many leaders are recognition addicts and want all of the credit. They spend too much time breaking-down rather than building-up their teams.

They do not take the time to genuinely learn about other's needs. Leadership is ultimately about knowing the people you serve and giving them the guidance, inspiration and navigational tools to make their lives better and enable more opportunities.

The Leadership Advantage

Leaders earn respect when they reward and recognize their Associates and colleagues. They take the time to appreciate and understand the unique ways they each think, act and innovate – and are always on the lookout to enable their talent. They are trusted, admired and respected because they make it more about the advancement of others, rather than themselves. They share the harvest of the momentum they build with others.

Earning respect is a journey and requires leaders to focus on how they can "deliver beyond what is expected" of their role and responsibilities. It is about always being on the look-out for ways to improve and being mindful of ways to make the workplace better and the organization and its people more competitive and relevant.

The following diagram summarizes the personal goals you should pursue to enable *Respect* to play a role in helping you maximize your Leadership Advantage.

The Leadership Advantage

Average Level of Respect	Maximum Level of Respect
You feel that you naturally respect others, but you never challenge the congruency of your view of respect and your leadership style.	You believe that respect is an important value and that this view helps to create a culture of respect within your team and the entire organization.
You normally think of respect as a feeling and a judgment about other people, even though you know this view can create a source of separation and conflict.	You understand that respect is a determination on your part of "who another person is" and should be separate from judgments you might have regarding their behavior.
You believe that you are owed some level of respect just because of where you are positioned on the organizational chart.	You know that you are not owed a level of respect simple because of your leadership role. You work at gaining the respect of others.
You work hard at maintaining an acceptable "work brand" that is separate from your personal brand.	You know that the most respected leaders are the most authentic people.
	The Leadership Advantage

131

"Respect yourself and others will respect you."

— **Confucius,** *Chinese teacher, editor, politician, and philosopher*

CHAPTER TEN

LEADERSHIP AND
FOCUS

"You can't depend on your eyes when your imagination is out of focus."

— **Mark Twain**, *American author and humorist*

The Leadership Advantage

We all have some ability to direct our attention to events and activities when it is apparent that there is a need or a problem. However, do we have the natural instinct or sufficient skill to ensure that the proper focus is always where it needs to be?

As we all know, becoming an effective leader is not a one-time thing. It takes time to learn and practice all of the required leadership skills. However, according to psychologist Daniel Coleman, "staying focused turns out to be one of the most important leadership skills"

In terms of leadership, when we speak about being focused, we commonly mean thinking about one thing while filtering out distractions. But a wealth of recent research in neuroscience shows that effective leaders focus in many ways, for different purposes, drawing on different neural pathways. Some paths seem to work in concert, while others tend to stand in opposition.

One way to shed new light on the practice of this essential leadership attribute is by grouping the *modes* of focus into the following three areas:

- ¤ Focusing on Yourself;
- ¤ Focusing on Others; and
- ¤ Focusing on the Wider World.

Focusing inward and focusing constructively on others helps us, as leaders, cultivate the primary elements of emotional intelligence. A deeper and broader understanding of how we focus on the *wider world* can improve our ability to develop strategy, innovate, and manage organizations.

In order to realize our maximum Leadership Advantage, we should cultivate this triad of awareness, in abundance and in the proper balance. Based on my experience, a failure to focus inward can leave you rudderless; a failure to focus on others can render you clueless at times; and a failure to focus outward may leave you blindsided.

In this chapter we will briefly explore these three *modes of focus* to help you understand how they work independently and how they together.

Focusing on Yourself

As most of us are aware, emotional intelligence begins with self-awareness and getting in touch with our inner voice. Leaders who heed their inner voices can draw on more resources to make better decisions and connect with their authentic selves.

Hearing your inner voice is a matter of paying careful attention to internal physiological signals. These subtle cues are monitored by the *insula*, which is tucked behind the frontal lobes of the brain. Attention given to any part of the body amps up the insula's sensitivity to that part. Tune in to your heartbeat, and the insula activates more neurons in that circuitry. How well people can sense their heartbeats has, in fact, become a standard way to measure their self-awareness.

Gut feelings are messages from the insula and the *amygdala*, which the neuroscientist Antonio Damasio, of the University of Southern California, calls "somatic markers." Those messages are sensations that something "feels" right or wrong. Somatic markers simplify decision making by guiding our attention toward better options.

To be authentic is to be the same person to others as you are to yourself. In part, that entails paying attention to what others think of you, particularly people whose opinions you esteem and who will be candid in their feedback. A variety of focus that is useful here is *open awareness*, in which we broadly notice what is going on around us without getting caught up in or swept away by any particular thing. In this mode we do not judge, censor, or tune out. We simply perceive.

Leaders who are more accustomed to giving input than to receiving it may find this difficult. Someone who has trouble sustaining *open awareness* typically gets snagged by irritating details. Of course, being open to input does not guarantee that someone will provide it. Sadly, life affords us few chances to learn how others really see us and even fewer for leaders as they rise through the ranks.

Focusing on Others

The word "attention" comes from the Latin "attendere", meaning "to reach toward." This is a perfect definition of *focus on others*, which is the foundation of empathy and of an ability to build social relationships—the second and third pillars of emotional intelligence.

Leaders who can effectively focus on others are easy to recognize. They are the ones who find common ground, whose opinions carry the most weight and with whom other people want to work. They emerge as natural leaders regardless of organizational or social rank.

Having empathy, as a leader, is vital to your ability to focus on others. In order to appreciate the role empathy plays in leadership, we first need to have a clear understanding of what empathy means. Most times, we tend to confuse empathy with sympathy. We tend to believe that to be empathetic means agreeing or relating to the feelings another person has regarding a given situation or individual.

However, what empathy really means is being able to understand the needs of others. It means that you are aware of their feelings and how it impacts their perception. It does not mean you have to agree with how they see things. To the contrary, being empathetic means that you are willing and able to appreciate what the other person is going through.

We talk about empathy most commonly as a single attribute. But a close look at where leaders are focusing when they exhibit empathy reveals three distinct types. Each type is important to maximizing your Leadership Advantage. Here is a brief explanation of the three categories.

The first type is called *Cognitive Empathy*. Cognitive empathy is the ability to understand another person's perspective. Cognitive empathy enables you to explain yourself in meaningful ways— a skill essential to getting the best performance from your direct reports. Contrary to what many might expect, exercising cognitive empathy requires you to think about feelings rather than to feel them directly.

The Leadership Advantage

The second type is called *Emotional Empathy*
Emotional empathy is the ability to feel what
someone else feels. Emotional empathy is important
for effective mentoring, managing clients and reading
group dynamics. According to experts in the field,
*"emotional empathy springs from ancient parts of the brain
beneath the cortex—the amygdala, the hypothalamus, the
hippocampus, and the orbitofrontal cortex—that allow us to
feel fast without thinking deeply."* These parts of the brain
seem to "tune us in" by arousing in our bodies the
emotional states of others. It is widely believed that
emotional empathy can be developed.

The third type is called *Empathic Concern.*
Empathic concern is the ability to sense what another
person needs from you. Empathic concern, which is
closely related to emotional empathy, enables us to
sense not just how people feel but what they need
from you.

Focusing on the Wider World

Leaders with a strong outward focus are not
only good listeners but also good questioners. They
are visionaries who can sense the far-flung
consequences of local decisions and imagine how the
choices they make today will play out in the future.
They are open to the surprising ways in which
seemingly unrelated data can inform their central
interests.

Getting Them All to Work Together

Certainly as a leader you do not want to end up similarly compartmentalized. So, getting all three *modes of focus* to work together is the key to being a truly focused leader.

You should not just focus on being the leader known for concentrating on the three most important priorities of the year, or the most brilliant systems thinker or the one most in tune with the corporate culture. You must be able to command the full range of your own attention:

- You are in touch with your inner feelings;
- You can control your impulses;
- You are aware of how others see you;
- You understand what others need from you; and
- You can weed out distractions and also allow your mind to roam widely, free of preconceptions.

That is when you realize your maximum level of Leadership Advantage.

The following diagram summarizes the personal goals you should pursue to enable *Focus* to play a role in helping you maximize your Leadership Advantage.

The Leadership Advantage

Average Level of Focus	Maximum Level of Focus
You consider yourself focused when you think about one thing and just filter out distractions.	You know that staying focused is one of your most important leadership skills and that your focus naturally spans a number of pathways.
You focus primarily on yourself and what you need to achieve. You consider others only when it is beneficial.	You know that focusing inwardly as well as on others can help you cultivate the primary elements of emotional intelligence.
You hear your inner voice frequently but ignore it most of the time.	You know that hearing your inner voice is a matter of paying careful attention to internal physiological signals.
You believe that being empathetic means agreeing with the feelings of others and that empathy has no place in your role as a leader.	You utilize your empathy as a leader to enhance your constructive focus on others.
	The Leadership Advantage

Leader-In-You

Leader-In-You

Honestly answer each of the following questions either with *Yes*, *No* or *Do Not Know*. The following *Selfish-Food-For-Thought* Section provides advice regarding evaluating your responses.

	Yes	No	D-N-K
1. I am present and in-the-moment during interactions, physically, intellectually, and emotionally.			
2. I am congruent in words, voice, face, body, and emotion when communicating.			
3. I actively empathize with others, and can put myself in their shoes, seeing and feeling things as if from their point of view.			
4. I maintain a regular process of self-reflection, an opportunity for introspection and reconnection with what is most important.			
5. I connect with my audience through appropriate and relaxed use of eye contact, vocal variety and projection, gesture, and movement.			
6. I listen to what is being said, as opposed to thinking about what to say in response			
7. I consider and respond appropriately to the needs, feelings and perspectives of different people in different situations.			

The Leadership Advantage

8. I am familiar with my own personal leadership values, and am able to clearly and passionately articulate them.			
9. I actively eliminate distractions and "noise" from interactions with others (e.g., turning away from the computer during important telephone conversations).			
10. I am tactful, compassionate and sensitive --- I treat others with respect.			
11. I vary my expressiveness based on the situation, appropriately conveying authentic emotion and passion.			
12. I base my actions and words on my own values and those of my organization.			
13. I listen for and acknowledge others' strengths and values, and, when appropriate, share my positive insights regarding what they have said			
14. I am flexible and spontaneous, adapting behavior and work methods in response to new information, changing conditions, or unexpected obstacles.			
15. I am aware of my energy level and mood when communicating, as well as the effect of my energy and mood on those around me.			
16. I respond appropriately and authentically in difficult situations.			
17. I accurately read the physical, verbal, and emotional cues of others with whom I am communicating.			
18. I articulate clearly and get to the point quickly.			

The Leadership Advantage

19. I seek ways to convey openness and to find common ground with others.			
20. I have and project self-confidence, inspiring and leading others through my actions as well as my words.			
21. I understand the intent of my message: what I want the listener to do, think, feel and/or understand when I am done communicating with them.			
22. I say "Yes" to and acknowledge the contributions of others, generously and wholeheartedly.			
23. I maintain a regular practice of relaxation (e.g., exercise, yoga meditation, etc.), to help maintain my physical and emotional balance.			
24. I build strong, lasting relationships based on trust.			
26. I use language effectively and creatively, applying the power of metaphor, imagery, stories, and examples to galvanize my audience.			

The Leadership Advantage

Selfish-Food-For-Thought

Selfish-Food-For-Thought

Selfish-Food-For-Thought provides advice based on the results of your responses from the Leader-In-You exercise. If you did not have at least 14 answers as *Yes* or *No*, you should consider taking another honest go at the exercise. Most leaders will have responses that are skewed one way or the other.

If you answered 14 of more questions as "Yes"

Your responses indicate that you possess a rare ability to remain centered, focused, open, and relaxed when facing the tensions and distractions of modern life. Your high self-assessment on this dimension also suggests that you maintain a heightened awareness of yourself and others in leadership interactions. In dealing with change, you possess a good deal of spontaneity, and are able to cope well when unexpected fires appear. You approach people and situations with generosity and calm, rather than with anxiety. As someone who is strong in this dimension, you are a natural model for others, effectively enhancing qualities of awareness and openness in those you work with.

The Leadership Advantage

You are someone with a natural ability and inclination to empathize, connect, and build relationships. You have a strong aptitude for listening and make authentic connections based on your genuine interest in other human beings. As a communicator, you reach beyond individual roles and work functions to a personal level of relating. You are not afraid to share of your own experiences as a way to bond and portray who you are as a leader while simultaneously looking to highlight the value that others bring to the table. You probably have an affiliate management style, letting those who work for you know that there is someone who cares, someone who is focused on more than just the work.

If you answered 14 of more questions as "No"

Your responses indicate some potential challenges in the area of being Present. You may be too busy, distracted, tense, or not mentally "in the room" with those whom you are trying to communicate with. This can present challenges and not only in terms of the presence you convey—it may also impair your ability to fully listen to others and to have complete understanding of their needs. The silver lining is that by becoming aware of this now, you have the opportunity to improve. For example, adding a regular, daily practice of centering and relaxation to your life would be of enormous benefit.

The Leadership Advantage

If you are short on time, even taking a quick walk around the parking lot when you feel foggy or turning away from your computer to do some breathing will help.

Your own assessment indicates a lack of comfort in the area of Expressiveness. This is not unusual: public speaking is considered by many to be their greatest fear. However, the downside of not being expressive when leading or motivating others can be significant. The ability to effectively express yourself in a business context will certainly improve your chances of engaging and inspiring others.

Observing what makes others successful in this area may be a good first step toward improvement. Who do you know who is an engaging, believable presenter? What do they do that works so well? How do they change their voice and use gestures to match the story they are telling? Getting feedback is also important. Ask a trusted co-worker to offer some positive feedback as well as constructive criticism after your next meeting. Look at the details: What is working well? How would they suggest you improve your use of vocal variety (are you a bit monotone?), your body language, and your use of images, metaphors, and stories to convey your points?

IN CONCLUSION
Doing More.
Leading More.
Earning More.

The Leadership Advantage

Y ou have achieved many hard earned professional and personal victories along the trail you have taken to reach the current position you hold in life. As a leader, you have spent countless hours studying, practicing and perfecting your craft. However, the question is *"Are you in the position to earn all that the world has to offer you and are you equipped to do more and lead more in order to earn it?"*

I believe that the answer is "yes." Because you have taken the time to understand this new interpretation of leadership and the unbridled potential of your *Leadership Advantage;* and because you have cognitively consumed the succinct messages in each of the ten chapters of this book regarding the relationship between leadership, the *Ten Absolute Attributes* and your instinctive ability to leverage this unique potential…you are now in the position to do more, to lead more…and to earn more.

As one of the greatest champions and athletes of our times, Michael Jordan, once said *"Some people want it to happen, some wish it would happen, others make it happen."*

I challenge you to go…*make it happen.*

About The Author

Since 2010, Earl has been the CEO and Managing Partner of Richer Life, LLC --- a digital media, trade book publishing and professional services company, headquartered in Phoenix. He spent the previous 34 years of his career in Fortune 100, Mid-Market and Venture companies as a Systems Engineer, Program & Project Manager, Management Executive and Technology Executive.

Earl has held executive management positions with *Motorola*, *The Reynolds & Reynolds Company* and *Wells Fargo Bank*. Earl is the former President, COO and CEO of the high-tech start-up, *MedContrax*.

He earned a Bachelor of Science degree, with honors, in Electrical Engineering from Tennessee State University and graduated from Arizona State University with the degree of Master of Science in Engineering. He is a former Adjunct Professor of Management at the Keller Graduate School of Management of DeVry University.

Earl is the author of five published books, including his bestselling book, *Focused Leadership: What You Can Do Today to Become a More Effective Leader.*

ǂRICHER Press
An Imprint of Richer Life, LLC

RICHER Press is a full service, specialty Trade publisher whose sole goal is to *shape thoughts and change lives for the better.* All of the books, eBooks and digital media we publish, distribute and market embrace our commitment to help maximize opportunities for personal growth and professional achievement.

To learn more visit
www.richerlifellc.com.

www.ingramcontent.com/pod-product-compliance
Lightning Source LLC
Chambersburg PA
CBHW032002190326
41520CB00007B/330